Thou Shalt Not Kill

A Plea for Life

TRANSLATED WORKS OF PIERRE VIRET

The Catechism of Pierre Viret

The Christian and the Magistrate

Defend the Truth: a Conversation on the Ninth Commandment

Honor thy Father and Mother

Letters of Comfort to the Persecuted Church

No Other God: A Practical Look at a Personal God

Nothing Like God: A Penetrating Application of the Second Commandment

Remember the Sabbath Day

Simple Exposition of the Christian Faith

Taking His Name in Vain

Thou Shalt Not Commit Adultery

Thou Shalt Not Covet

Thou Shalt Not Steal

For a full listing of available titles, please visit:
psalm78ministries.com

Thou Shalt Not Kill

A Plea for Life

by Pierre Viret

with a sermon by John Calvin

Translated by R. A. Sheats

Psalm 78 Ministries

www.psalm78ministries.com

Thou Shalt Not Kill: A Plea for Life

by Pierre Viret, with a sermon by John Calvin

Translated by R. A. Sheats

Published by:

Psalm 78 Ministries
P. O. Box 950
Monticello, FL 32345

www.psalm78ministries.com

ISBN: 978-1-938822-58-2

Printed in the United States of America.

Biblical quotations are taken from the King James Version of the Holy Scriptures. Divine pronouns have been capitalized.

FRONT COVER PHOTO CREDITS:
Sleeping Newborn Infant, Andrés Nieto Porras, wikicommons
ICU IV 1, Calleamanecer, wikicommons
US Supreme Court, Mr. Kjetil Ree, wikicommons

TABLE OF CONTENTS

Translator's Note

Thou Shalt Not Kill: A Plea for Life is an English translation of a portion of Viret's commentary on the Ten Commandments, published originally in 1564 in French under the title *Instruction Chrestienne en la doctrine de la loy et de l'Evangile*, and printed in Geneva by Jean Rivery.

With the intention of presenting his readers with an easily-understood, down-to-earth exposition of the Ten Commandments, Viret wrote his commentary as a conversation between two fictitious characters, Daniel and Timothy. *Thou Shalt Not Kill* breaks into the middle of this conversation as Timothy and Daniel begin to discuss the meaning and application of the sixth commandment.

Unless otherwise noted, Scripture quotations are taken from the King James Version of the Holy Bible. Where Viret cites Scripture but does not quote verbatim, his wording has been retained and the Scriptural reference placed in parentheses. Chapter breaks and headings do not appear in the original, but have been added for ease of comprehension. Scripture references in brackets have also been added by this translator.

The final two chapters of *Thou Shalt Not Kill* are taken from a sermon preached by John Calvin on December 21, 1555. This sermon was given as he was preaching through the book of Deuteronomy. The text is derived from Arthur Golding's English translation of Calvin's sermons published in 1583 under the title *The Sermons of M. John Calvin upon the Fifth Book of Moses* (printed by Henry Middleton for

Thomas Woodcocke, London). Archaic words, phrases, and grammatical structures have been updated for the sake of clarity and better understanding. Chapter breaks as well as headings within the chapters have been added.

CHAPTER ONE

The Sixth Commandment and Anger

"Thou shalt not kill."

— Exodus 20:13

THE PURPOSE WHICH THE SIXTH COMMANDMENT AIMS TOWARD, AND THE UNITY AND CONJUNCTION IT HAS WITH THE PRECEDING COMMANDMENT

TIMOTHY: When you spoke of the order which the Lord gave to the commandments of the second table and the matters contained in them, you also declared what the sixth commandment dealt with, which is the second commandment of the second table, which declares: "Thou shalt not kill" (Ex. 20:13; Deut. 5:17). Since the Lord gave a law concerning the duty and position of those under authority to their superiors by which He also sufficiently instructs those in authority of their duty and position toward those under their charge, He also in this commandment gives a law concerning the preservation of the life and person of every man.

DANIEL: You have remembered well what we already discussed concerning this matter. On this you must note that, just as there is one position in the world of those who beget, nourish, and raise children, so there is also another of those who are born, nourished, and raised. And as this second cannot exist without the first (of which we spoke in the preceding commandment), so also the first, which is the first source of mankind and of human society and life, cannot be maintained or preserved unless this commandment is in place. Therefore this preservation is here commanded us in this commandment, in which the life of each one of us is not only commended in general, but also in particular. For the many cannot be preserved without the individual, of which it is composed, as a body of many members. Therefore whoever takes the life of one man is rightly judged an enemy of the entire human race and of all human society in general. For if we individually take each man one after another, we will not fail in the end to constitute the entire human race.

Thus this commandment is quite properly commanded after the preceding one. For, seeing that God wills that we honor those by whom He has given us life and by whom He preserves us in it, and that He promises a long and blessed life to those who obey the commandment He gave, it is quite reasonable, seeing that life is such a good gift of God, that all consider the preservation of it as very precious and very valuable to all. And in commending to us the life that we have received from our parents in this manner, He also commends to us those from whom we have received it, admonishing us that we must hold them as dearly as we do the gift we have received from them.

THE TRUE SENSE OF THIS COMMANDMENT, AND THE EXPOSITION JESUS CHRIST GAVE OF IT

TIMOTHY: This reminds me of what you said concerning the sense and understanding of the Law. Because of this, though God only specifies murder in this commandment, yet I do not doubt that this law also encompasses all the internal sins and desires from which murder proceeds, or which are linked to it.

DANIEL: It is just as you say, as our Lord Jesus Christ quite clearly declared when He said: "Ye have heard that it was said by them of old time, Thou shalt not kill; and whosoever shall kill shall be in danger of the judgment: but I say unto you, that whosoever is angry with his brother without a cause shall be in danger of the judgment: and whosoever shall say to his brother, Raca, shall be in danger of the council: but whosoever shall say, Thou fool, shall be in danger of hell fire" (Matt. 5:21-22). By these words we can easily see that the Lord not only forbids the outward act, but also the evil affection from which it proceeds, no matter whether it is concealed or revealed before men.

It should come as no surprise that God, who is a Spirit and desires to be worshiped "in spirit and in truth," requires such an observance of His Law, and that He punishes the wicked affection which He sees quite clearly, seeing that even human civil laws themselves punish not only the wicked act, but also the wicked will and the wicked intention when it reveals itself by some wicked signs and when it proceeds as far as to display some effort to put it into execution, even though the act might not be fully executed. For the Law is "the Word of God," derived from the nature of Him from whom it proceeds. Therefore by necessity it must be "quick, and powerful, and sharper than any two-edged sword, piercing even to the dividing asunder of soul and spirit, and of the joints and marrow, and is a discerner of the thoughts and intents of the heart" (Heb. 4:12; Eph. 6:17).

THE MEANING OF THE EXPOSITION JESUS CHRIST GAVE OF THIS COMMANDMENT, AND PARTICULARLY WHAT HE SAID ABOUT BEING ANGRY WITH ONE'S BROTHER, AND THE PENALTY OF IT

TIMOTHY: Seeing that our Lord Jesus Christ Himself

explained this law, we need go no further to seek a better expositor of it. But I do not quite understand the full meaning of His words which you quoted.

DANIEL: You must understand, firstly, that our Lord Jesus never sought to alter this law against murder. Nor did He seek to add to it or diminish from it. But, because the entirety of the Law of God had been corrupted by the false understanding and false expositions of the scribes and Pharisees, He desired to restore it in its entirety and return it to its true meaning, by which He clearly shows that we must understand and receive His law in the sense that we have said. And for this reason, desiring to make us understand how this law of murder must be applied not only to the outward act but also to the desire and affection of the heart, He begins at the original source and root—the heart—which produces such fruit.

For, before a man arrives at such great hatred and cruelty as to take the life of his brother and destroy the image of God in which he was formed, it is quite certain that he must have firstly conceived some envy, hatred, and grudge against him. Thus he follows what James said: "the wrath of man worketh not the righteousness (or justice) of God" (James 1:20). This was apparent in Cain, who first conceived an envy and hatred against his brother, and then nourished it until it clearly revealed itself in the murder committed against his brother (Gen. 4:1-8).

Now our Lord Jesus declares that when a man has already proceeded as far as this wrath and hatred, he is considered a murderer before God, in whose judgment such a wicked heart is counted more wicked than murder and homicide are esteemed in the eyes of men. And therefore He places this act in the same degree as murder, saying that such a man will be in danger of judgment. For the word does not mean that he will actually be punished, but that he is worthy of punishment, meaning that he deserves condemnation before

God if his sin is not cleared by His mercy to those who request pardon. Therefore John said: "Whosoever hateth his brother is a murderer: and ye know that no murderer hath eternal life abiding in him" (1 John 3:15). For the same reason it is also said in Leviticus: "Thou shalt not hate thy brother in thine heart. . . . Thou shalt not avenge, nor bear any grudge against the children of thy people" (Lev. 19:17-18). By this we can truly see that the exposition that our Lord Jesus gives of this commandment quite clearly has its foundation in the teaching of Moses himself.

ANGER RESTRAINED, AND HOW WE CAN BE ANGRY WITHOUT OFFENDING GOD; AND THE SENSE WHICH JESUS CHRIST TAKES: "WHOSOEVER IS ANGRY WITH HIS BROTHER WITHOUT A CAUSE," AND THE THINGS TO BE CONSIDERED IN THIS MATTER TO PROPERLY DISCERN BETWEEN A HATRED DIRECTED AGAINST PERSONS FROM THAT WHICH MUST BE DIRECTED AGAINST SINS

TIMOTHY: I understand this well. But what does the rest of what our Lord added to this first level of murder mean?

DANIEL: After a man has in this way conceived some envy, hatred, or grudge in his heart against his brother which incites him to revenge and to do him some wrong, if he manages to restrain it, he is not as guilty as if he nourishes it and gives it a free rein. This is why Paul said: "Be ye angry, and sin not: let not the sun go down upon your wrath: neither give place to the devil" (Eph. 4:26-27).

TIMOTHY: It seems that Paul desires us to understand by these words that you can be angry without sinning.

DANIEL: There are two ways by which we can be angry without offending God. The first is when we are concerned with considering, restraining, and chastening our own sins more than those of others, and that, knowing the vileness of our sins, we are grieved and angry with ourselves, and turn against ourselves the wrath that we pour out against the sins of others.

TIMOTHY: I would find this manner of anger quite good; but we are not often angry in this way.

DANIEL: The other is when we see God offended and when, being moved by a true zeal and desire for His glory and the good of our neighbor, we are enraged against whoever commits such a crime, not out of hatred for his person, but for his sin, hating the sin which is of the devil, and hating the devil in it, not the person created by God, in order that we might not hate God in him.

TIMOTHY: I believe that Paul indeed allows us to be angry in both these ways.

DANIEL: So also does our Lord Jesus Christ. This is why He did not simply say: "whosoever is angry," but He also added "with his brother." For if we are justly angry, it is not against our brothers—that is, against their person, such that the brotherhood that we must have together be broken—but we are angry at the sin and at Satan who dwells within them, whom we must not receive as our brothers, but as our mortal enemies.

The word "without a cause" is also added, which some (and particularly Jerome) say is not necessary, and was not added by Jesus Christ or the Evangelist, because it is not found in [some of] the oldest and most correct copies of the New Testament.[1] Therefore, it seems that this might have been added as an explanation, and that it might have been transposed from the margin where it had annotated the text.

[1] In his commentary upon this passage, Calvin says nothing of this doubt.

But whether it was or not, it is no cause for much concern. If it is a part of the text, we must take it as an interpretation of what is said; if we let it pass, what we have said of the word *brother* will satisfy all, for the sense remains the same.

TIMOTHY: It is true.

DANIEL: Now we must note two things on this. The first is that, though we might have a just cause for anger against someone because of his sins, yet we are not often angry out of a zeal for the glory of God, but we instead become angry out of our hatred for the person because of the offense he committed, and in order that we might execute our own revenge under the guise of the glory of God, instead of acting out of a hatred for the sins which are in it.

The other is, though our anger is just and is founded on a very good cause, we must beware of mixing our personal desires with it, which might trouble us and drive us beyond the limits of reason, charity, and justice. These are the two things against which Paul also warns us.

TIMOTHY: Both of them truly merit our careful thought, for there are few who do not commonly err in this regard.

ANGER PROCEEDING FROM A MINOR CAUSE OR ANGER WHICH IS IMMODERATE IN A JUST CAUSE, AND THE REMEDY AGAINST IT

DANIEL: We must also consider that we are often moved quite strongly against very minor causes, by which we again err greatly. Thus if, instead of growing angry against sin, we err by growing angry against persons, it follows that, though we may have a good reason for being angry, yet our sin is still much greater as much as the cause of the anger is much lighter. And the sin is even worse if we have no good reason, either light or otherwise. And if, besides all this, man is not content to have been moved in anger other than he ought to be, but to the contrary nourishes this anger in his heart and leaves it there concealed in such a way that it proceeds to the boiling point and thus reveals itself by some outward sign, this always renders him much guiltier.

TIMOTHY: Because of the infirmity of our human nature in which we are born, it is very difficult to be able to moderate our desires and emotions in such a way that they do not often proceed further than the bounds, not only of what is lawful, but also of what we ourselves would wish.

DANIEL: It is true. But when this happens, if we cannot heed the first rule that Paul gave us which we already mentioned, we must endeavor at least to follow the other which he immediately adds, and use the remedy he proposes to us, saying: "Let not the sun go down upon your wrath: neither give place to the devil" (Eph. 4:26-27). By these words he admonishes us that, if we have been moved to anger and have grown wrathful for any other reason or in any other way than what we have said, we must deal with ourselves as quickly as possible and beware of harboring our anger within ourselves until the morning.

TIMOTHY: This is a very good remedy.

HOW THE EVIL ONE ENTERS OUR HEARTS AND TAKES POSSESSION OF THEM THROUGH WRATH AND ANGER; AND THE DILIGENCE WE MUST HAVE OF CHASING HIM AWAY, AND THE BEST MEANS OF DOING THIS

DANIEL: And, to better encourage us to do this, he shows us the danger that we place ourselves in if we are negligent of this, by what he adds: "neither give place to the devil." For we must not doubt that the anger he speaks of proceeds from the devil, and that the devil cannot capture our heart except when we retain this anger. Therefore it is not said without cause: "An evil man seeketh only rebellion; therefore a cruel messenger shall be sent against him" (Prov. 17:11). Thus it is indeed safest for us to drive the anger away from us as quickly as we can. For, if we allow it to reside within us for a long time, it will take such possession of us that we will not be able to easily dislodge it when we wish to. For it is very difficult to uproot such an inveterate and deep-seated root from our hearts, as we can daily see from experience. Therefore above all things we must fear lest this seed take root within us.

TIMOTHY: Not without reason; for if the devil takes possession of our hearts by means of wrath and anger, we ought to truly fear lest such a guest lodge and remain with us for a long time. There are none who would not take great pains if they realized that they had a thief staying in their house with them with the intent to plunder and rob them; or that an outlaw was waiting to slit their throat; or an arsonist waiting to set fire to the house and consume all within it. I do not think there is any man who would sleep peacefully and at ease while he knowingly accommodated such guests in his home, and who would not immediately seek every means possible to find a way to chase them out of his house. Yet the devil is much more dangerous than these. Therefore it is quite necessary for us to strive to chase him so far from us that not only can he not lodge with us, but he cannot even approach us.

DANIEL: This would be much better.

CHAPTER TWO

Degrees of Murderous Anger

THE SMOLDERING OF ANGER MENTIONED BY JESUS CHRIST, AND HOW WE LET THE SUN SET UPON IT; AND HOW ALL WRATH AND ANGER IS MADNESS

DANIEL: When the sun extends its rays over the earth, it heats all upon it, but when it withdraws in the evening, the heat that it kindled and enflamed is cooled. We must do the same with our anger after it has become enflamed. We ought to send it to bed with the sun and return to our right minds, which were carried away by it; for wrath is accompanied by madness. Therefore, as long as a man is moved by wrath, he is carried away from understanding like a madman. And there is no difference between a madman and an angry man except that the madness is of a shorter duration in one of them. Nevertheless it is always madness. Therefore, as long as wrath remains, so long also madness is a resident.

TIMOTHY: Then it was not without good reason that it was formerly said by some pagan that it would be good for an angry man to look at himself in a mirror while he is angry, for this would greatly assist him by showing him how much his anger had altered his face. And to see himself assume such ugly and terrifying grimaces would recall him to moderation, for he would be as horrified at himself as much as at a savage beast.

DANIEL: To speak the truth, a man overcome with anger (in a manner of speaking) is a man no longer, but is as it were transformed into a savage beast. This is also the reason why the Spirit of God so frequently uses comparisons taken from brute beasts to describe anger, wrath, cruelty, and the other wicked affections of men by which these transformations of men into beasts are customarily accomplished.

TIMOTHY: If you were to ask a man whether he would like to be turned into a savage beast (or be transformed into any beast at all), I do not doubt that he would hold this in great horror and would find it much against his nature.

DANIEL: Doubtless so. And yet there are very few indeed who fear that this will truly happen to them, being transformed by their emotions, just like insane beasts.

Now to return to where we began, our Lord Jesus Christ shows us that He judges the smoldering of anger to be worthy of punishment by the council, saying: "whosoever shall say to his brother, Raca," and "whosoever shall say Thou fool shall be in danger of hell fire." He previously declared what punishment a man deserves before God who "is angry with his brother without a cause" (Matt. 5:22). Now if this crime is already so grievous, it is even further aggravated when we nourish anger within our heart and leave it to smolder as the sun sets, contrary to Paul's warning (Eph. 4:26). For we ought indeed to content ourselves with having already offended God by being moved to anger without a cause, without giving any further rein to it, as if we were pleased with it.

WHAT IT MEANS TO SAY "RACA" TO A BROTHER, AND TO "BE IN DANGER OF THE COUNCIL;" AND OF CONCEALED AND REVEALED ANGER

TIMOTHY: What you say is true, but I do not understand

what this word *Raca* means. Nor do I understand the reason for the difference Jesus Christ places between the one who says "Raca" and the one who says "Thou fool" to his brother.

DANIEL: When a man, moved by anger, does not follow the advice given us by Paul, it is quite certain that he will not be able to conceal this internal fire which he covers and leaves smoldering in his heart in such a way that some spark or flame will not shoot out, or at the very least a little smoke. It is impossible for him not to show himself to be angry, spiteful, and contemptuous against his brother, but he will reveal this anger, vexation, and contempt by some words and signs which reveal the wickedness and the devil which lie hidden in his heart.

We have examples of all this in the first place in Cain, the first murderer and the first son of the devil. For, by what the Lord said to him: "Why art thou wroth? and why is thy countenance fallen?" it is plainly revealed to us that his countenance and face were a clear witness of the enmity hidden in his heart (Gen. 4:6). And didn't Esau say in his heart: "The days of mourning for my father are at hand; then will I slay my brother Jacob"? (Gen. 27:41.) And how many times did Saul, being angry with David, purpose in his heart to put him to death, and even attempted to kill him with his own hand? (2 Sam. 18:6-11, 29.) Wasn't David himself so carried away with his anger that he would have killed Nabal if God had not prevented him by the wisdom of Abigail the man's wife? (1 Sam. 25:32-35.) Thus we can see how anger grows and blossoms.

Now if a man does this by hidden words and signs of indignation, as by sour faces and mutterings, without declaring it fully, he says *Raca* to his brother. For our Lord Jesus Christ seeks to make us understand by this word *Raca* (which has no certain meaning), all these signs of which we have just spoken, and this second degree of anger which has not yet proceeded to the highest degree. And therefore He said that the crime of the man who allows his anger to proceed this far without restraining it is considered by God as guilty as murder, and a crime of which the offender would be already fully convicted in such a way that there is no further need of a trial in judgment, which a criminal is still admitted to in his defense because he is not fully convicted of his crime. Or it would be as a crime which is considered so grievous before men that the judge must consult, not to advise if it must be considered a crime or not and if it merits punishment, but to deliberate upon the manner of punishment, and to find some appropriate sentence to mete out a vengeance such as it requires.

THE THIRD DEGREE OF WRATH AND ANGER MEANT BY THE NAME 'FOOL,' AND THE PUNISHMENT OF HELL AGAINST IT AND ALL THE OTHERS

TIMOTHY: I understand this point well enough. Let us proceed to the other.

DANIEL: If anger proceeds even further, in such a way that it boils over to the highest degree and proceeds to open outrage against whomever it is enflamed, He places this as a desperate condition worthy of a greater punishment than men can imagine, as are those of hell and eternal fire; as if God in thunder and lightning gave the sentence from His exalted heavenly throne with His angels.

TIMOTHY: Why did our Lord Jesus Christ choose to express this third and final degree of anger by the name *fool?*

DANIEL: Because He means an obvious offense, by which we must not only understand that He condemns those who use such an insult against their brother, but also all those in general who proceed as far as this great anger and who insult their brothers by this in whatever way they may; and particularly those who use curses and execrations. For when a man curses another, he openly declares that, if he had the power, he would willingly do what he wishes upon him. When he curses a man by wishing him an unnatural death or by sending him to the devil, he openly declares that he would willingly kill him if he dared and was able to, or that he would literally send him to hell if he had the power to do so. Isn't this a very clear testimony by which he shows himself a very obvious murderer—not only of the body but also of the soul—and that nothing but a lack of power hinders him from the actual accomplishment of the deed?

TIMOTHY: The matter is quite clear. But why is it that our Lord Jesus only declared these people to be "in danger of hell fire"? Don't the others who grew angry and who harbored their anger as we have said, though their rage didn't burst forth as these did, also deserve eternal damnation before God?

DANIEL: They most certainly do. But our Lord speaks in this way for the reasons I have already stated, and to make us understand that punishment in hell will also be given according to the nature of each one's sins.

TIMOTHY: You wish then to say that all those who are punished with eternal damnation are not only in everlasting torment, but that some will be more grievously tormented than others.

DANIEL: You can truly see that Jesus Christ did not say without reason that the inhabitants of the cities of Sodom and Gomorrah will be more gently treated in the Day of Judgment than those who have despised and refused the grace presented to them by the preaching of the Gospel, and that the servant who knew his master's will and did not do it will be beaten with more stripes than he who neither knew nor did it (Matt. 16:27; Luke 10:13-15; 12:47-48). He would have spoken this senselessly if there were no differing degrees of punishment according to the magnitude of the sins.

TIMOTHY: That makes sense.

CHAPTER THREE

Brotherly Reconciliation and Lawsuits

THE FINAL DEGREE OF MURDER; AND THE CONSIDERATION WE MUST HAVE OF JESUS CHRIST'S WORDS; AND OF THE DANGER INTO WHICH HATRED AND WRATH LEAD US

DANIEL: Now if Jesus Christ judges anger worthy of so grievous a punishment when it proceeds so far, what will become of those who are not content with injuring their brother by words, but proceed as far as violence and striking and killing?

TIMOTHY: Men scarcely ever think of these things, but to the contrary they consider them much more lightly than does our Lord Jesus Christ.

DANIEL: Yet the judgment will not be made according to their estimation or opinion, but according to the sentence Jesus Christ gave here. Therefore all ought to truly think differently than they have done, and pay heed to what Paul says: "Let all bitterness, and wrath, and anger, and clamour, and evil speaking, be put away from you, with all malice: and be ye kind one to another, tenderhearted, forgiving one another, even as God for Christ's sake hath forgiven you" (Eph. 4:31-32).

TIMOTHY: This would truly be the best thing. Jesus Christ indeed shows us here how this devil remains in us whom Paul admonishes us to not give place to. For if we give place to him and permit him to lodge under our roof, he will not fail to reimburse us with a payment for the lodging we gave him. And he will not abandon us if he can help it, until we lodge with him in the boardinghouse of hell and eternal fire which is assigned to him and all of his (Matt. 25:41).

BROTHERLY RECONCILIATION, AND THE NEED THAT WE HAVE OF IT; AND HOW WITHOUT IT WE CANNOT OFFER PRAYERS OR ANY OTHER WORK PLEASING TO GOD

DANIEL: We must not doubt this. Therefore after Jesus Christ thus expounded the law of murder, immediately following His exposition He adds an exhortation toward brotherly reconciliation, saying: "Therefore if thou bring thy gift to the altar, and there rememberest that thy brother hath ought against thee; leave there thy gift before the altar, and go thy way; first be reconciled to thy brother, and then come and offer thy gift" (Matt. 5:23-24).

Our Lord Jesus said these words while the sacrifices commanded in the Law were still in place in the church of Israel. Now there was nothing in all the divine service which was at that time held in greater esteem than the sacrifices, which were figures and were like illustrations and sermons of the great Sacrifice which had to be made by our Lord Jesus Christ. Despite this, our Lord Jesus, to better instruct us all how much hatred and wrath displease God, and how much love and brotherly kindness please Him, expressly said that we must never hope to offer a sacrifice pleasing to God while we bear some hatred and wrath against our brother, until we be restored to grace, friendship, and unity with him.

TIMOTHY: Now that we no longer have such sacrifices and

such altars and offerings as the Jews had previously, how can we apply this teaching?

DANIEL: If we recall what was said of the offerings, we can apply this very well to all the works which God requires of us, which are like sacrifices of praise—particularly prayers, almsgiving, and the partaking of the sacraments (Heb. 13:15).

For we cannot do any work pleasing to God unless we ourselves are first pleasing to Him. For, properly speaking, our works (which by nature cannot be pleasing to Him) cannot render us pleasing to Him, but they are rendered pleasing when the persons from whom they proceed are pleasing to Him—which they cannot be of their own nature, except by means of Jesus Christ His well-beloved Son. Now while envy, hatred, and wrath dwell within us (and the devil also by means of them), Jesus Christ cannot dwell with us, without whom however we can never be pleasing to God, but only greatly displeasing and detestable.

Therefore if we are in such a state and we address ourselves to Him either by prayer or by some other work in His praise, He will speak to us as He did to the hypocrites against whom Isaiah prophesied: "And when ye spread forth your hands, I will hide Mine eyes from you: yea, when ye make many prayers, I will not hear: your hands are full of blood" (Is. 1:15). And in another place: "your iniquities have separated between you and your God, and your sins have hid His face from you, that He will not hear. For your hands are defiled with blood, and your fingers with iniquity; your lips have spoken lies, your tongue hath muttered perverseness" (Is. 59:2-3).

Certainly our hands are defiled with blood if we are murderers and manslayers. Now we cannot deny that we are murderers and manslayers according to the judgment of the Word of God when we bear hatred and bitterness against our brothers, as we have already shown.

TIMOTHY: I think this is the reason why Paul, as though thinking of the words of Isaiah, said: "I will therefore that men pray every where, lifting up holy hands, without wrath and doubting" (1 Tim. 2:8).

DANIEL: It is quite certain that our hands are not holy when they are stained with blood, which they are when there is wrath and discord within us. For this same reason (as the Lord Himself testifies by His prophet Isaiah) He despised the sacrifices, prayers, and all the works of bloody men (Is. 1:11-15).

THE CARE WE OUGHT TO TAKE OF AVOIDING LAWSUITS AND OF SEEKING RECONCILIATION WITH EACH OTHER; AND THE DANGERS IN WHICH MEN WHO PURSUE LAWSUITS PLACE THEMSELVES

TIMOTHY: It seems to me that in another place He also said the same of the fasts and repentance of those who have quarrels and who go to court against their brethren, and who press them without pity or compassion (Is. 58:3-5).

DANIEL: You raise a point which our Lord Jesus Christ also expressly mentioned in the passage we are dealing with when, immediately after what I just quoted regarding brotherly reconciliation, He said: "Agree with thine adversary quickly, whiles thou art in the way with him; lest at any time the adversary deliver thee to the judge, and the judge deliver thee to the officer, and thou be cast into prison. Verily I say unto thee, thou shalt by no means come out thence, till thou hast paid the uttermost farthing" (Matt. 5:25-26; Luke 12:58-59).

Our Lord Jesus Christ shows us by His first exhortation which He made of brotherly reconciliation that we cannot be reconciled to God or find favor in His sight if we are not firstly reconciled with our brothers. For how dare we open our mouth to speak even the beginning of the prayer that our Lord Jesus taught us, and say "Our Father which art in heaven," if we do not receive as brothers those whom God receives as His children like us—that is, if we do not bear them brotherly love? Again, how dare we say "Forgive us our sins; for we also forgive everyone that is indebted to us," if we do not forgive them at all?

In the second exhortation He warns us of the dangers to which quarrels and lawsuits can bring us, and teaches us by the physical damages which can ensue what spiritual damages we shall receive. For, besides the fact that it is difficult to engage in a lawsuit against someone without anger, bitterness, and ill will by which God is greatly offended, there is also a grave danger of failing in our case before the judge; for often those who think they have a strong case are greatly deceived. And, no matter how just the cause might be, it always stands in great danger when it comes before the judgment of men because of both the ignorance and the corruption and iniquity within them. Therefore it is always safest and most profitable to settle before going to the rigors of the law, for when you proceed that far, there is no further place for reconciliation, but rather the utmost severity.

HOW THIS COMMANDMENT REQUIRES US TO FORGIVE OUR ENEMIES AND NOT TO RESIST EVIL

TIMOTHY: If what you say happens in the judgments of men themselves, we can truly understand what judgment will befall those who present their case before God when they would not be reconciled with their brethren during this life while they were in this way, and when they had the opportunity to do so.

DANIEL: It will happen to them as it did to the servant Jesus Christ speaks of in the parable, who never forgave his companion or showed him any mercy, but pursued him to the fullest extent of the law. Therefore he was measured with the same measure he used toward his brother (Matt. 18:28-35).

TIMOTHY: If we truly considered these admonitions and warnings, we would have fewer quarrels, dissentions, lawsuits, and court cases than we do, and we would spare no expense to obtain peace, no matter what it might cost us.

DANIEL: However, if we do not do this, we do not fulfill this commandment of God: "Thou shalt not kill," according to the sense and exposition that Jesus gave of it.

TIMOTHY: I understand this well.

CHAPTER FOUR

Private Revenge and God's Vengeance

DANIEL: It would be much better for us to follow what Jesus Christ commands us immediately following what we already quoted: "Ye have heard that it hath been said, An eye for an eye, and a tooth for a tooth: but I say unto you, that ye resist not evil: but whosoever shall smite thee on thy right cheek, turn to him the other also. And if any man will sue thee at the law, and take away thy coat, let him have thy cloak also. And whosoever shall compel thee to go a mile, go with him twain" (Matt. 5:38-41; Ex. 21:24; Deut. 19:21; Lev. 24:20; Luke 6:29). This agrees well with the remonstrance that Paul made to the litigants among the Corinthians, admonishing them to suffer wrongs and injuries rather than take their brother to court, as they were doing—indeed, even before unbelieving judges (1 Cor. 6:1-7).

THE SENSE IN WHICH THE WORDS OF JESUS CHRIST MUST BE TAKEN BY WHICH HE FORBIDS RESISTING EVIL, AND THE PERSONAL VENGEANCE FORBIDDEN BY GOD

TIMOTHY: These laws would truly burden us severely if they must be understood according to the literal meaning of the words. But I do not think we ought to understand them so. For our Lord Jesus Christ Himself, being struck by an officer, did not turn the other cheek to be struck a second time, but reproved the man who struck Him of the wrong that he did to Him (John 18:22-23).

Paul also, after Ananias the high priest commanded him to be struck, not only did the same as Jesus Christ his Master, but rebuked and much more strongly reproved him who commanded such an injustice to be committed (Acts 23:2-5). Yet I do not think that Jesus Christ violated His own teaching, or Paul, either.

DANIEL: You must not think otherwise. Therefore these two examples can serve as an exposition of this passage. Thus, when Jesus Christ commands us to offer the left cheek to those who strike the right and also to give our cloak to whoever takes away our coat (and the rest that follows this same purpose), He does not wish by this to force us to seek out more evil than what our enemies have done to us; but He wishes to make us understand that the perfection of the Law requires not only that we not touch the person of our neighbor to do him wrong either by word or deed and that we bear no enmity or hatred against him without reason, but even more, it requires that though we have been wronged and injured first, we must not return evil for evil. But we must instead be prepared to endure a double injury rather than cause a single one and begin to avenge ourselves by our own actions and on our own authority for what has been done to us.

Paul declares this in very clear words, saying: "See that none render evil for evil unto any man; but ever follow that which is good, both among yourselves, and to all men" (1 Thess. 5:15). And again: "Dearly beloved, avenge not yourselves, but rather give place unto wrath: for it is written, Vengeance is Mine; I will repay, saith the Lord" (Rom. 12:19; Deut. 32:35; Heb. 10:30). This is why in Psalms He is called the "God to whom vengeance belongeth" (Ps. 94:1). Thus let us end with what Solomon says: "Say not thou, I will recompense evil; but wait on the LORD, and He shall save thee" (Prov. 20:22).

THE REASONS WHY GOD HAS FORBIDDEN VENGEANCE TO PRIVATE CITIZENS, AND WHY HE HAS GIVEN THE CHARGE TO RULERS AND MAGISTRATES

TIMOTHY: Why has God reserved this office to Himself?

DANIEL: Because it is a right of the ruler, which pertains to him alone. Therefore, seeing that He is our sovereign Ruler and Lord, we must not think that He wishes to have any less right and authority in this point than earthly rulers do. Now you know that we ourselves are not permitted to mete out justice as private individuals, or to avenge ourselves for the wrongs which have been done us, but that this office is reserved to the magistrates and to those to whom the administration of justice has been committed. Therefore, if a man endeavors as a private citizen to accomplish for himself what an officer must do for him, he will be arrested by justice as having usurped an office which in no way pertains to him.

TIMOTHY: It is true, and the reason for it is also good. For, if it were lawful for every man to judge his own cause and to execute his own sentences, there would be no justice in the world at all, but instead a public slaughterhouse in which the strongest would always uphold his own case. For the love that we each have for ourselves is the reason why we cannot see clearly, either in our own right, or in the rights of others. Self-love is also why we always prefer to do injury to others rather than ever requiring a recompense of ourselves. Therefore it is quite reasonable that men other than ourselves, who are not driven by such affections, should have the knowledge and the judgment in these matters.

DANIEL: This is why God ordained rulers, magistrates, judges, and officers of justice, and why He gave them laws in order that they might regulate justice according to them; and why He so strictly commanded them to have no respect of persons nor to allow themselves to be swayed by their own emotions or desires, but that they judge with righteous judgment (Deut. 1:12-17). Thus, since He (who is the Sovereign of all) has established this order, whoever attempts to break and confound it is worthy of great punishment. Thus if rulers—who are no more than God's proxies—will not endure to have anyone usurp their office except those to whom they have given such a charge, we must not think that God, who is much greater than they, will endure the same done against Him.

HOW THERE ARE NONE TO WHOM THE EXECUTION OF VENGEANCE UPON THOSE WHO MERIT IT MORE CLOSELY AFFECTS THAN GOD, AND HOW NONE BUT HE ALONE ARE ABLE TO FULLY AND PERFECTLY EXECUTE THE WORK

TIMOTHY: You wish then to conclude that we must leave to Him the vengeance of the injuries which have been done to us.

DANIEL: Isn't this more than reasonable? For, as vengeance pertains to Him and not to any other, so also none have such courage to work justly as He does, nor indeed can any do so, for many reasons.

The first is because no harm or injury can be committed which does not first and foremost offend the majesty of God. Therefore the sin committed does not touch us only, but touches Him even more closely than us, because there is no sin at all unless His majesty and commandment are violated. Thus we must not think that He will leave it unpunished, for He knows much better than we do how to judge properly, and what punishment it merits.

The other reason is that no one has the power to execute vengeance upon whoever did the injury except Him alone. For, firstly, which is it that has done us an injury: the body or the spirit of our enemy?

TIMOTHY: It is certain that the body is no more than the instrument of the spirit. Therefore the evil which is done by it proceeds from the wicked spirit which leads and governs it. Thus it follows that the body is like the sword, and the spirit like the one who handles and wields it.

DANIEL: Seeing that it is so, man cannot then avenge himself of his chief and greatest enemy, but only of his enemy's weapons and armaments, and not even that when he wishes. For, if his enemy is more powerful, he cannot do anything, but instead of avenging himself upon him, he himself would receive a new injury. And though he might find himself more powerful than his enemy, yet the enemy might find many means of concealing himself and placing himself in security, and so escape from his hands. Therefore there is no man, no matter how great a ruler he might be, who always possesses the power to avenge himself of all his enemies in their bodies, or even only in their goods.

But God is He alone who can take vengeance both upon the body and the soul, and "destroy both soul and body in hell" (Matt. 10:28). For He is the Lord both of the body and goods, and of souls and spirits, and possesses a limitless domain in both heaven and earth, to whom all creatures are subject. Therefore nothing can escape from His hand. To the contrary, though He tarries, yet all shall one day appear "before the judgment seat of Christ; that every one may receive the things done in his body" (2 Cor. 5:10; Rom. 14:10).

HOW THE BEST MEANS TO AVENGE ONESELF OF ONE'S ENEMIES IS BY ENDURING AND LEAVING THE VENGEANCE TO GOD; AND HOW HE WHO SEEKS TO AVENGE HIMSELF DOES MORE HARM TO HIMSELF THAN TO HIS ENEMY

TIMOTHY: Seeing it is so, we thus cannot do better than to patiently endure the wrongs which are committed against us, and leave all vengeance to Him.

DANIEL: There is no other means as sure as this. For He will do it much better than we, whereas if we seek to carry it out ourselves against His command, we will transform our good cause into an evil one, and will provoke Him to anger and vengeance against ourselves by the wrong we commit against His majesty. Thus we will not obtain anything which is not more to our damage than to the damage of our adversaries. For, if the worst comes to the worst, we will work against our own body and goods and, in seeking to work against their body and goods, we will work against our own soul, not only when we actually put into execution what we desire, but even if we only have the desire to do it though we do not possess the power to carry it into execution. Who then is more harmed by this hatred and vengeance: he who wreaks vengeance upon someone, or he upon whom it is wrought?

TIMOTHY: It is easy to judge by what you have said. Thus I conclude that there is no better means for us to take our revenge against our enemies to our profit and without any damage, than to simply place all our causes in the hand of God.

DANIEL: It is certainly true. For if it pleases Him to punish in this world those who have done us wrong, it will be easy for Him to do so either by the magistrates and officers He has ordained to do this, or by any other means that please Him. For this reason our Lord Jesus Christ taught us to avenge ourselves of our enemies by patience, and to vanquish them by this means, saying: “In your patience possess ye your souls” (Luke 21:19); not by giving them an advantage over us to injure us more and more, but in removing their opportunity of doing so.

THE MEANS BY WHICH WE CAN PREVENT OUR ENEMIES FROM HARMING US AND BY WHICH WE CAN RECONCILE THEM TO US; AND THE TEACHING AND EXAMPLES OF JESUS CHRIST AND HIS APOSTLES IN THIS MATTER

TIMOTHY: How can this be done?

DANIEL: By choosing rather to suffer injury (as we have already said) by doing and rendering them good for evil, rather than in taking vengeance against them for what has been done to us. For, in seeking to avenge ourselves, we always further incite our enemy against us, as well as committing an offense against God.

TIMOTHY: Is this what Jesus Christ says about turning the other cheek, giving away our cloak, and going further than is required of us? (Matt. 5:39-41.)

DANIEL: You can judge by what He Himself did. For when He was struck and insulted, He was not moved with anger. Nor did He curse His adversaries or render them wrong for wrong, but instead good for evil (John 18:22-23). As Peter said, He "committed Himself to Him that judgeth righteously," as he also commanded us to do. Paul likewise declared: "Be not overcome of evil, but overcome evil with good" (1 Pet. 2:19-23; Rom. 12:21). Therefore it follows in this same chapter in which Jesus Christ expounds the Law: "But I say unto you, love your enemies, bless them that curse you, do good to them that hate you, and pray for them which despitefully use you and persecute you; that ye may be the children of your Father which is in heaven: for He maketh His sun to rise on the evil and on the good, and sendeth rain on the just and on the unjust" (Matt. 5:44-45). And Paul, to this same purpose: "if thine enemy hunger, feed him; if he thirst, give him drink: for in so doing thou shalt heap coals of fire on his head" (Rom. 12:20; Prov. 25:21-22).

Though our Lord Jesus Christ did not literally turn the other cheek to the man that struck Him, yet He did not do anything against what He taught, but instead fulfilled it, just as He wills that it be fulfilled in us; for He employed the patience to which He calls us, without giving way to any wrathful outbursts at all. He still further displayed this when He restored Malchus' ear and when He, being in greatest agony, prayed for those who crucified Him (Luke 22:50-51; 23:33-34; John 18:10-11). By His actions He showed how these words must be understood.

THE RESPONSE PAUL MADE TO ANANIAS THE HIGH PRIEST, AND THE DIFFERENCE BETWEEN IT AND THAT WHICH WAS MADE BY JESUS CHRIST IN NEARLY THE SAME CIRCUMSTANCES, BOTH TO THE JEWISH COUNCIL AND BEFORE PILATE, AND THE REASONS WHY

TIMOTHY: It seems to me that we cannot say the same of Paul's action that I already mentioned, for he spoke more sharply to the high priest than Jesus Christ did against a lowly servant (Acts 23:2-4).

DANIEL: On this we must consider that, though Paul upheld the cause of Jesus Christ, yet he was called to perform another office than what Jesus Christ was called to fulfill when He was put to death for us. For this was the time when it was necessary for Him to be humbled and cast down beneath all men, and to be presented before the judges as guilty instead of us, and as a criminal who remains silent before his judge, being convicted; just as we would have to be presented before the judgment of God if He by this means had not exempted us. For this very reason, when He was taken not only before Pilate, but also before Caiaphas and the high priests and their council,

He offered no response at all to what was said against Him, though He could have responded, having been wrongfully accused, struck, and beaten (Ps. 38:10-15; Matt. 26:59:63; John 19:8-9).

But another purpose existed in the case of Paul. He was there for the defense of his ministry. Therefore he represented not a private individual, but a public person and a prophet and ambassador of God. Therefore he had just reason to show to this hypocrite who, under the title of God's name and justice, contravened all justice, how he was unworthy of such an office, and what wrong he did to God by so basely abusing His name; as also our Lord Jesus Christ so sharply rebuked the scribes and Pharisees when the occasion demanded it (Matt. 23:13-36). And because the cowardice of this tyrant was more insupportable than the sin of the servant who struck Jesus Christ because of the person whom he represented, it was much worthier for Paul to "answer a fool according to his folly, lest he be wise in his own eyes," in order that he might know himself (Prov. 26:5).

And furthermore, seeing that this hypocrite so villainously abused the name and the holy throne of God, he truly deserved to have his hypocrisy brought to light and to be sharply reproved for the dishonor he rendered to God, and to have the judgment which God had prepared for him pronounced against him by Paul His servant. Therefore we must not consider Paul's words as a wrong proceeding from anger, but as a Christian reproof and correction.

CHAPTER FIVE

The Broad Scope of the Sixth Commandment

THE POINTS REQUIRED BY JESUS CHRIST FOR THE FULL OBSERVANCE OF THIS COMMANDMENT, AND THE REASONS WHY GOD CHOSE TO SET FORTH IN IT THE VICES WHICH ARE CONTRARY TO HIM, RATHER THAN THE LOVE WHICH IS THE TRUE OBSERVANCE OF IT

TIMOTHY: I have no further difficulty concerning this point. But it seems to me that the declaration that Jesus Christ made concerning this commandment calls us much further, and requires a very great perfection of ourselves, from which we are all far removed.

DANIEL: It is true. For firstly, He forbids us from being the first to work an injury.

Secondly, after we have received one, not only must we not render the same to our enemies, but we must also patiently endure it. Then we must be prepared to do more than our adversaries require of us in an attempt to restore peace, rather than do anything contrary to our calling.

Furthermore, He also desires that we not only guard ourselves from rendering insult for insult, but also of bearing hatred against those from whom we have received the injury (Lev. 19:18; 20:7).

And, not content with this, He further requires that we

love our enemies, that we seek their good in every way, and that we pray for them (Matt. 5:44). For John indeed did not say: "Whoever *hates* his brother abideth in death," but "He that *loveth not* his brother" (1 John 3:14). And therefore it was not without reason that the Lord chose to forbid the sins against this commandment rather than command the love which "is the fulfilling of the law," as it is also of all the rest of the Law, according to Paul's testimony (Rom. 13:10; 1 Tim. 1:5).

For within His law He follows the order and the means which the vinedressers and laborers of the earth follow in their labors. For, before planting their good seed and their good plants in the earth which they cultivate, they first remove the evil plants and uproot and burn them. For if they did otherwise, what fruit could they expect from their seeds and plants sown and planted among such rocks, thorns, weeds, thistles, and other evil plants and herbs, without having firstly cultivated and prepared the earth as is necessary?

Thus, seeing that the hearts of men are like fallow ground, and so full of rocks and thorns because of the natural corruption and wicked desires and vices which have taken such deep root within them that they cannot be uprooted, it is indeed necessary for the Lord to begin to pluck up before He plants, and to destroy the work of the devil before He builds His own, following what was spoken by Jeremiah: "Break up your fallow ground, and sow not among thorns. Circumcise yourselves to the Lord, and take away the foreskins of your heart" (Jer. 4:3-4).

Thus, after we have truly cleared and emptied our hearts of the rocks and thorns of hatred, enmity, grudge, and other wicked roots and seedlings of murder and manslaughter, we must plant in their place the good plants of love and brotherly kindness, and bear the fruits of them, each one toward his brother. Therefore it is not enough to say: "I do not wish him any evil; I just leave him alone," but you must go beyond this and seek his good, and declare this by works, and exert yourself on his behalf.

For if we do not proceed this far, even though we may endure all harms both to our bodies and goods—indeed, the removal not only of our goods, but also of our very life—without being moved to wrath, hatred, and vengeance, yet we do not fulfill this law. For if we refrain from working evil against those who do us no harm, the savage and vicious beasts do the same. And can it be that a beautiful Christian perfection proceeds no further than the savage beasts in virtue? And if we only do good to those who do the same to us, as our Lord said: "What do ye more than others? Do not even the publicans so?" (Matt. 5:47.)

And if the Lord who gave the Law does not require in it any other perfection of His people except that they refrain from murder and manslaughter, how is His Law different from any other law of human lawgivers—even of the pagan lawgivers—who have given laws to their people? For there are none, not even of the most barbarous peoples and nations that have ever been, who not only condemn murder and manslaughter, but also judge that murderers and manslayers must not be endured among men upon the earth, but to the contrary are unworthy of being allowed to live.

THOSE WHO RENDER EVIL FOR GOOD; AND MURDERS, AND THE LAWS GIVEN AGAINST THEM

TIMOTHY: If we cannot fulfill this commandment without accomplishing all these things toward our very enemies, it then follows with an even greater force that we cannot satisfy it if we do not do the same toward all, and that it is not only required of us to keep ourselves from doing harm to our neighbors, but also that we labor for their good by all means possible for us. Now if this commandment extends so far, we can truly judge how those must displease God who render evil for good, and above all murderers and manslayers who in fact kill and murder men instead of doing them good and acknowledging the goods which have been done them and giving their own life to preserve theirs.

DANIEL: It is said of the first: "Whoso rewardeth evil for good, evil shall not depart from his house" (Prov. 17:13). Concerning the others, the laws that God gave against such people declare well enough in what esteem He holds them. For He has commanded: "He that killeth with the sword must be killed with the sword," and: "He that killeth any man shall surely be put to death," and that: "Whoso sheddeth man's blood, by man shall his blood be shed: for in the image of God made He man" (Rev. 13:10; Lev. 24:17; Gen. 9:6; Ex. 21:12). This Law was again confirmed by Jesus Christ when He commanded Peter that: "All they that take the sword shall perish with the sword" (Matt. 26:52; John 18:11).

The reasoning that the Lord added to this, concerning His image in which men were created, is well worthy of consideration. For if someone desecrated and ripped up or broke the coat of arms of some king or ruler, no matter what realm or domain they might be, how great a crime would they consider this? Would it not be punished, not only as a murder, but also as a crime of high treason, as if the majesty of the ruler and the realm had in fact been desecrated?

TIMOTHY: This is also a crime which truly merits grievous punishment because he who commits it not only declares what contempt but also what hatred he bears in his heart for the ruler and the country which the coat of arms represents, because in doing this he spites them and gives an example to others to do the same, and brings confusion upon public order and human society.

DANIEL: Seeing that it is so, how should we regard those who desecrate, ruin, and destroy the image of God? How much greater punishment do they deserve?

THE REVELATION OF THE VAST CORRUPTION AND PERVERSITY WITHIN HUMAN NATURE WHICH IS SHOWN BY THIS LAW AGAINST MURDER, AND THE BROAD SCOPE OF THIS COMMANDMENT

TIMOTHY: These laws and commandments given against murder make me think of the vast corruption and perversity which is within men by nature, and of the great power that the devil, that murderer of old, has over them because of sin. For is there any cruelty more bestial and which can scarcely be found in any living creature except man, than to kill him who is of his own species and his own flesh and blood, and made in the image of God? Are there any beasts so ferocious, savage, fanatical, or so vicious, which being of the same species, kill and devour each other as much as man does? For, though the beasts are not partakers of reason so as to understand that this is neither just nor equitable, nevertheless the common nature that they have among themselves and which governs them teaches them to have some regard for their own kind and some recognition of the natural unity that they have among themselves.

Therefore we can rightly say that murderers and manslayers despise all nature, and must be taken for monsters among men. But even if this had never happened and we had never experienced what we so frequently see, the Lord quite clearly declares by His Law that man possesses this cruelty within his very nature. For, if it were not so, He would not have given such laws.

DANIEL: He also warns us of this corruption in all the other commandments and laws He gave us.

Now you should also note the generality of this commandment and these laws, both with regard to the persons who can kill or be killed, as well as the times and means by which homicide can be committed. For He does not say, "So-and-so cannot kill so-and-so," or cannot kill a certain number, or at a particular time in a particular place by whatever instrument or means it may be, but He forbids all—without any exception—to kill anyone at all, whoever they might be, at whatever time, in whatever place, by whatever instrument or means at all. I understand this of a man killing by his own authority and desire, without being called by God to execute His vengeance.

TIMOTHY: This is truly something to be considered.

HOW THE LORD DID NOT EVEN ALLOW MEN TO KILL THOSE WHO WERE IN THEIR SERVICE AND POWER, AND HOW HE GAVE A LAW TO THIS SAME EFFECT AGAINST BEASTS AND BY FORBIDDING THE DRINKING OF BLOOD; AND THE REASON FOR IT

DANIEL: The Lord even expressly gave a law against masters concerning their servants, ordering that if the masters struck them in such a way that they died under their hand, they were to be punished (Ex. 21:20). And what is even more, He not only gave this law against men who murdered, but also against beasts which killed someone.

And, in order to place homicide in the greatest horror and to further dissuade men from it, He forbade the ancients from drinking even the blood of beasts; giving them to understand by this how precious we ought to consider the blood of man, and to guard against the shedding of it; seeing that He desires us to hold in horror even the blood of beasts which have been given to man as meat by God's express permission (Gen. 9:3-4). For it seems that this drinking of blood has some type of cruelty in it. And we must not doubt that whoever has learned to be humane toward beasts will show himself even more considerate toward men.

TIMOTHY: You remind me of what God so often repeated to the Jews by the prophets, of having violated this command as if they had committed a truly abominable crime. Indeed, when speaking of the state of the Church which would exist at the coming of Jesus Christ, He says by Zachariah that "I will take away his blood out of his mouth," (Zech. 9:7). By this we can see that He had some thought to what you just said. For it is quite certain that He has a greater concern for the reason why He gave this law than to the external and ceremonial keeping of it.

DANIEL: What you say appears reasonable. For even when God gave this law we just quoted against murder, He most clearly declared that He has a greater regard for the blood of men than for that of beasts. And just as the prophet Isaiah prophesied that savage beasts will graze with domesticated animals, signifying the change which will occur in the hearts of men by the preaching of the Gospel (by which, being regenerated by the Spirit of God, they will be as it were transformed from beasts into men), we can also indeed say truly that the blood is removed from their mouth when their cruelty is changed into humanity and Christian love (Is. 11:6-7; 65:17-25).

THE LAW GIVEN AGAINST BEASTS GUILTY OF MANSLAUGHTER AND AGAINST THEIR OWNERS, AND AGAINST ALL THOSE WHO ARE AN ACCESSORY TO THE MURDER BECAUSE THEY DID NOT TAKE PRECAUTIONS AGAINST IT

TIMOTHY: This law against beasts which you just mentioned is still observed today. For if a beast has killed a man or a child, justice executes it as a criminal. Now concerning this I consider that, if God commanded that even beasts (who are without reason and understanding) were not to be excused in such a case, but to the contrary were to be judged worthy of the judgment due to manslayers and murderers, what excuse will man (to whom God has given understanding and reason) find before the judgment of God if he slays his brother who was created in the image of God like himself? And will it be any more excusable for the judge who excuses him?

DANIEL: It is easy to judge. And because beasts have neither sense nor understanding like man does, God's law does not only require the punishment of the beast that killed, but also that of its owner if he already knew that the beast was dangerous and had not taken precautions for restraining it as he ought (Ex. 21:28-32). For his negligence is in part the cause of the murder committed by the beast. By this the Lord teaches us that not only the murder and the one who did the actual deed is displeasing to Him and is judged by Him as worthy of death, but also all those who do not employ all diligence in taking precautions against the murder, as is also clearly shown by this other law in which the Lord says: "When thou buildest a new house, then thou shalt make a battlement for thy roof, that thou bring not blood upon thine house, if any man fall from thence" (Deut. 22:8). He said this because in those days the roofs of the houses served as rooms, as also appears in the Gospel according to Matthew, where He commanded the apostles: "what ye hear in the ear, that preach ye upon the housetops" (Matt. 10:27). It was also said of David that he "walked upon the roof of the king's house" (2 Sam. 11:2). We must also understand this law to apply to all dangerous places where our brethren could be harmed or killed.

CHAPTER SIX

Murders Committed by Words, Assistance, or Approval

THOSE WHO SHOW FAVOR TO OR APPROVAL OF MURDER IN ANY WAY, AND WHO ARE THE CAUSE OF IT, AND WHO DO NOT SEEK TO BRING PEACE TO ALL AND TO BE A PEACEMAKER BETWEEN THOSE WHO ARE IN DISAGREEMENT

TIMOTHY: What then must we say of those who not only fail in this regard, but who also aid, abet, and show favor or approval to the murderers, in whatever way they might do it, and who were a cause of it?

DANIEL: It is easy to judge this matter.

TIMOTHY: If whoever did these things deserved the full sentence of a murderer, there would be few men indeed who would often involve themselves in these matters. For we will find precious few exemptions, even for those who provided nothing more than evil counsels and evil connections by which men are daily placed and supported in angry strife against each other, which is often the cause of many murders and deaths, or at least of great hatreds and quarrels.

DANIEL: It is true. Therefore we must truly beware of this.

For, though the murder might not have been committed by our hand, yet if we are the cause of it in any way at all, it is all the same or little less than if our hand had done the deed itself.

But what is even more, it often happens that whoever is the instigator of the murder or the abettor of it, is much guiltier than he who actually committed the deed with his own hand. For many who commit murder would never do so if they were not induced to it by others. Therefore Solomon, when speaking of the six things which the Lord hates, did not only list "hands that shed innocent blood," but also the "heart that deviseth wicked imaginations," and "feet that be swift in running to mischief." Then he added a seventh, which was a grievous abomination to Him: "he that soweth discord among brethren" (Prov. 6:16-19).

Thus we must judge the same of angry strife, dissensions, and violent disagreements; for it is not enough for us to simply refrain from doing these things, but we must also beware of encouraging others to do so. And at the same time we must labor to restore peace between those who are at odds, in order that we might be those of whom it is said: "Blessed are the peacemakers: for they shall be called the children of God" (Matt. 5:9).

VARIOUS MEANS BY WHICH MEN CAN BE MURDERERS BY THEIR WORDS OR BY SIGNS AND OTHER MEANS WHICH ACCOMPLISH THE SAME AS WORDS

TIMOTHY: I understand by what you have just now explained concerning this matter that there are three ways in which men can be murderers: by works, by words, and by heart. I also understand how they can be so by heart and work, but I would like you to explain to me a little better what types of murders can be committed by words.

DANIEL: Firstly, all those who give counsel to kill the innocent and anyone whom it is not lawful to kill, kill by their words; as Herodias killed that holy man John the Baptist when she counseled her daughter to request his head, and Herod was persuaded by this to kill him (Matt. 14:6-11; Mark 6:17-28). We can say the same of all those who are today in the counsel of rulers, who by their counsel persuade them to persecute the Church and kill the faithful and innocent. We could add to these not only those who give such counsel (as are today the popes, cardinals, bishops, priests, and monks), but even more so those who, being in the office of counselors or assistants and judges of justice, condemn them by their sentences of judgment even as Pilate condemned Jesus Christ (Matt. 27:22-26), and as the members of the Inquisition and the counsels of the antichrist condemn the faithful and deliver them to the secular arm as heretics; just as the bishops, scribes, Pharisees, and the priests of Jerusalem delivered Jesus Christ, already condemned beforehand in their council, and particularly by the sentence of Caiaphas (John 11:47-50, 18:12-14, 19-24; Matt. 26:57-66).

They are also murderers by words who give the order to kill the innocent, whether they do it covertly or openly, as we have examples of in the commandment which Saul gave to David to battle against the Philistines in order that he might be killed by their hand and not by his; and likewise in what David did in commanding Joab against Uriah, in order to secretly kill him (1 Sam. 18:17, 25; 2 Sam. 11:14-17). Thus we see what covert or secret commands are.

There are others quite obvious, as that of Herod against John the Baptist and of all the tyrants against the prophets, apostles, and true martyrs and disciples of Jesus Christ; and that of Saul against the priests of Nob, and that of Jezebel against Naboth (1 Sam. 22:18-19; 1 Kings 21:7-13).

We can add to these all those who by betrayal deliver men to death, as Judas delivered Jesus Christ, and all those who accept bribes to kill the innocent, of whom it is written in the Law: "Cursed be he that taketh reward to slay an innocent person. And all the people shall say, Amen" (Deut. 27:25). Now if he who receives the gift is a murderer cursed by God, he who gives it and makes the bargain is no less guilty, but is perhaps even more so.

It is also written: "Cursed be he that smiteth his neighbour secretly" (Deut. 27:24). We can include under this manner of murder not only those who kill in secret either by sword or by poison, but also all false witnesses and all those who obey the murderous commands of tyrants to testify and pronounce a sentence of death against the life of the innocent to please the tyrants. This was done against Naboth by the citizens of his city, by which Micah's words were accomplished: "the prince asketh, and the judge asketh for a reward; and the great man, he uttereth his mischievous desire: so they wrap it up" (Micah 7:3).

THOSE WHO COMMIT MURDER BY AN ACCIDENTAL BLOW, NOT BY A DELIBERATE ACTION; AND THE EXEMPTION GOD ORDAINED FOR THEM, AND WHY HE DID SO

TIMOTHY: The man who deliberately commits murder or who approves of and gives his consent to it truly deserves the punishment we have spoken of. But what do you say of those who kill someone without premeditation, or accidentally, either in being attacked by their enemies or by an accident or unfortunate happenstance, against their desire or will?

DANIEL: Concerning those who kill ignorantly by accident, God has given an explicit law by which He grants them an exemption (Ex. 21:12-13). He does not exempt them from justice, but in order that violence might not be shown them by the relatives and friends of the slain before their cause is known and judged. If it is proven that the man who killed bore no enmity to the dead man, and if there is no reason to suppose that he who did the deed did it willingly, it is ordained by the Law that such a person be declared innocent (Num. 35:15, 22-25).

And, to give a better understanding of this Law, God set forth an example: "As when a man goeth into the wood with his neighbour to hew wood, and his hand fetcheth a stroke with the axe to cut down the tree, and the head slippeth from the helve, and lighteth upon his neighbour, that he die," even though the man with the axe in no way desired the death of the slain man (Deut. 19:5).

But if it is found in the trial and legal proceedings of the case that he bore the man any hatred beforehand, or had some occasion by which it is clearly revealed that whoever did the deed had been induced to do it voluntarily, there is no exemption for him if it is found that he has willingly murdered someone (Deut. 19:11-13; Josh. 20:1-9).

On this it seems to me that the example of accidental homicide which is set forth in the Law is worthy of note. For the Lord gives us a case which might happen by accident in performing a useful and necessary work, as is the labor commanded by it. But if such a case occurs either at play or while doing some other work which is done without any profit or good, which of its own nature would be wicked, it seems to me that there must be another consideration, in such that he who did the deed might bear some guilt. For it seems that God sometimes wills by this means to punish the laziness of idle men who do not know how to use their time except in games and foolishness.

TIMOTHY: And if it happened that a drunken man fell over another man in his staggering, and broke the man's neck, does it seem to you that he should be declared innocent simply because his action was not premeditated?

DANIEL: You can truly judge that he is guilty in this case, and deserves punishment. We can say the same of all other such cases in which there is some guilt of murder, even though the murderer never intended to murder.

THE SOURCE OF EXEMPTIONS, AND THE REASON FOR THEM, AND HOW THEY WERE ORDAINED FOR THE DEFENSE OF THE INNOCENT AND NOT FOR THE PRESERVATION OF THE WICKED OR THE OBSTRUCTION OF JUSTICE

TIMOTHY: I think that the exemptions which are still today assigned to murderers and other criminals were originally founded with a similar purpose and intention as these which were ordained in the Law, as you already said.

DANIEL: I agree with you; but there is a great abuse of them. For, instead of such exemptions serving to further justice, they scarcely serve for anything except the hindrance of justice. And, instead of protecting the innocent as they ought, they instead for the most part serve as a refuge for the wicked only, and give them boldness to wreak their violence and damage upon the good.

TIMOTHY: Did God never give such exemptions in His Law?

DANIEL: To the contrary, He expressly forbade them and had no desire for His temple to serve for such a purpose. For He commanded by express commandment that the murderer and deliberate manslayer must be removed from His temple and brought to justice according to His Law—indeed, even from "the horns of the altar," if he clung to them (Ex. 21:14; 1 Kings 1:50; 2:28).

Solomon executed this law against Joab after the death of David his father. For, though Joab was a close relative of David's, and though he had shown himself a good and loyal servant of the king all his life, and though he had brought great credit to the kingdom, and though he had fled for safety to the exemption found in the temple of the Lord, and was clinging to the altar, Solomon removed him from it to punish him for the murder he had committed in killing Abner by such a villainous treachery, as he had also killed Amasa (1 Kings 2:5, 28-34; 2 Sam. 3:27; 20:8-10).

THE ABUSES WHICH EXIST TODAY AMONG CHRISTIANS CONCERNING THESE EXEMPTIONS, AND PARTICULARLY IN CHURCHES AND MONASTERIES; AND THE LAW OF GOD GIVEN TO PURGE THE LAND IN WHICH A MURDER HAS BEEN COMMITTED WHEN THE PERPETRATOR IS UNKNOWN

TIMOTHY: This is indeed contrary to the exemptions which are now held among Christians. For the places most privileged in this way are the churches, convents, and cloisters of the priests and monks.

DANIEL: If the exemptions which exist among Christians benefited those who flee there by protecting them in order that no harm might befall them by the anger of individuals or by the tyranny and iniquity of wicked tyrants and judges until their case could be properly examined and handled according to true justice, they would be worthy to be maintained. But by creating a retreat, a hiding place, and a refuge for the wicked, and a hindrance to justice, I do not know how this can be in accordance with the Law of God. For God is gravely displeased when the crimes of men remain unpunished—particularly murder and manslaughter. For blood unjustly shed never ceases to cry out and demand vengeance (even as far as heaven itself, as that of Abel cried out against Cain) until justice is done (Heb. 12:24; Gen. 4:10). This is why it was ordained in the Law that if a body was found slain on some piece of ground and the murderer was unknown, it must be measured which city it was nearest to, and then it was ordered by express commandment that those of that city must request and make supplication to God, asking that He not impute this sin and this crime to their account, and that their land might not be soiled and polluted by it (Deut. 21:1-8). How then could a land be considered pure and clean in which the known murderers and manslayers are tolerated? For the shedding of human blood bears with it such a staining and pollution that it can scarcely ever be effaced and the land purged from it, and even less the hands which have been sullied and stained by it.

CHAPTER SEVEN

The Shedding of Blood

THE POLLUTION THAT THE SHEDDING OF BLOOD BRINGS WITH IT, AND THE HORROR THAT ALL MUST HAVE OF IT—INDEED, EVEN IN JUST CAUSES

TIMOTHY: Seeing that it is as you say, there are in the world today very few lands which are not heavily soiled with such stains, and in which there are precious few hands which have not been deeply infected.

DANIEL: Let us read what David said to his son Solomon: "My son, as for me, it was in my mind to build an house unto the name of the LORD my God: but the word of the LORD came to me, saying, Thou hast shed blood abundantly, and hast made great wars: thou shalt not build an house unto My name, because thou hast shed much blood upon the earth in My sight" (1 Chron. 22:7-8). And in another place: "But God said unto me, Thou shalt not build an house for My name, because thou hast been a man of war, and hast shed blood" (1 Chron. 28:3).

TIMOTHY: I am astonished at these words. For the wars which David fought and those he was engaged in, weren't they just wars and commanded by God? And didn't David fulfill his duty when he killed the enemies of the people of God just as God Himself had commanded in His Law?

DANIEL: He certainly did.

TIMOTHY: Why then didn't God want David to build Him a temple, as though He regarded David as soiled and polluted by the blood he had shed, even though he did it at God's command? If David had been a tyrant and a thief and a swindler (as are many military leaders and soldiers, who often engage in wars for their own profit), the reason for God forbidding him to build the temple would be obvious, or if God had forbidden it because of the unjust murder which he committed in the person of Uriah (2 Sam. 11:14-17). But He expressly mentions the vast amounts of blood that David shed in battle. By doing this it seems to me that God reproached David for something for which he ought to have been greatly praised, seeing that he never entered any war unless it was a just one and unless he entered it in his lawful office as a magistrate.

DANIEL: Though God did not wholly condemn David, and though He was honored by the wars he engaged in, yet He truly desired to make known that there is no war, no matter how just, in which He takes great pleasure, for many reasons.

Firstly, it is truly difficult to wage war so justly and righteously, and with men so humane and so righteous and just as they ought to be, in which there is not always much excess in many parts, particularly in the effusion of human blood and in which men bear some portion of wrath, revenge, cruelty, and other such wicked passions and emotions.

Secondly, as God is a God of peace, so also He holds wars in detestation as much as they are contrary to His nature. And this is why it is with great regret that He punishes men by such scourges. And therefore He does not employ them until man's wickedness and perversity has so greatly provoked Him to wrath and vengeance, when He is pressed so far that He must chastise them by such harsh rods.

Furthermore, because He created man in His own

image, human blood is very precious to Him. Therefore He wills that it be preserved as much as possible—indeed, even that of His enemies and of the most wicked. For this reason He considers as polluted and stained the hands of those who shed it, no matter how just the war might be. Thus, if the Lord holds blood in such esteem—even the blood of the most wicked of the earth—and considers it a horror to shed it, He clearly shows us by His example in what horror we ought to hold such shedding of just and innocent blood, and all other blood shed without His commandment and without a proper calling and jurisdiction.

TIMOTHY: If God did not desire David to build Him a temple because of the reasons you have set forth, but to the contrary commanded him to leave the charge to Solomon (who would be a peaceful king, as the Lord prophesied and promised to David), we can certainly understand how little pleasure He must take in the churches which have been erected among Christians, and of those who have built them. For how many are there which have not been built upon human blood, if we consider who the chief builders who constructed the building were? For how many of the most magnificent and most renowned structures were erected by kings and rulers out of the plunder and spoils and blood of the peoples and nations which were ruined and destroyed by their swords and arms? For it seemed to them that by these beautiful structures they would appease God for the blood they had shed and the injuries and violence they had shown to an infinite number of men and nations, and that these structures would also render their names immortal among men.

DANIEL: These beautiful edifices will serve them as a witness before God and men of the wrongs they have done to those whom they ought to have comforted, and of the blood they have shed. And if the Law of Moses of which we just spoke (concerning the dead body found in the fields) were observed, there would be few cities indeed among Christians which would not raise their supplications to God, not only for the murders in which the murderers are unknown, but also for those which are quite well known indeed.

THE DANGER IN WHICH RULERS AND OFFICERS PLACE THEMSELVES BY NOT PUNISHING MURDERERS AS THEIR OFFICE REQUIRES, AND WHO WITHOUT JUST CAUSE SHOW MERCY TO THOSE WHO DESERVE DEATH

TIMOTHY: This law truly shows us what danger men place themselves in—particularly rulers, judges, and their officers—when they leave known murderers and manslayers unpunished; or when they do not use such diligence as they ought in searching out and discovering them as they should; or when they flippantly show them mercy without a good or just reason to do so. For if those who are totally innocent must still fear lest the shed blood cry out for vengeance against them and their land be polluted and soiled with it, how much more ought those be afraid who are guilty because they have failed to fulfill the duties of their office?

DANIEL: You conclude quite well. For the judge who does not punish those whom he is charged to punish by the commandment of God his sovereign Ruler and Lord, renders himself guilty not only of the crime which the criminal has committed, but also of all those that he afterward commits, and also of the crimes of others who impudently engage in evil-doing because they see that wicked men escape without receiving a punishment worthy of their crimes.

TIMOTHY: We ought then to truly consider what diligence we must employ in the prosecution of such things, and on what considerations we can show mercy to criminals.

DANIEL: You speak truly. For if a subordinate judge commits some iniquity in judgment, either in condemning the innocent or in freeing the guilty or in showing him mercy against the will and desire of his sovereign ruler, it is quite certain that if the sovereign ruler is such a man as he ought to be, he will not fail to respond. Now when it is a matter of justice, those who are sovereign with regard to men are subordinate and subjects with regard to God, who alone is the Sovereign of all. Let them therefore carefully note that this is not only what they can do and what pleases Him, but it is what they must do, and what is lawful, just, and equitable for them; in order that they might not sin against justice either by a too great severity or by a too great license. For as there is a danger that too severe a judgment shall be found to be a great injustice, it is also greatly to be feared that too great a clemency and mercy shall indeed be found to be a great cruelty. For it is a very inappropriate and cruel clemency and overmuch mercy to take pity on wolves and therefore open for them the gate to the sheep, and allow them to devour them [Prov. 12:10].

TIMOTHY: Then you do not approve of kings, rulers, and magistrates who think themselves at liberty to show mercy to everyone they please without a good and just cause, and without any other reason besides their own pleasure.

DANIEL: I approve of all this just as much as they would approve such a liberty in each of their own officers and subjects, if of their own authority they showed mercy to every malefactor and criminal whom their sovereign rulers had condemned to death by their laws and edicts.

TIMOTHY: Yet there are few kings, rulers, and lords who show any great difficulty in doing this when they are constrained by persons, or for persons whom they favor. And what is even worse, far from considering that they have violated their office and duty in such a case, to the contrary they think they have rendered a great service to God by showing mercy to the worst criminals in the world, as is clearly evident by the fact that they have consecrated a certain Friday to this work which, after the manner of the Roman Church, is called "The great and holy Friday," and "Good Friday," which they regard as the holiest day in all the year. For if there is any hope at all of obtaining mercy, indeed even for the wickedest man in the world, it is on this day. What do you say of this custom?

DANIEL: I say that they consecrate this holy day exactly like the Jews consecrated their feast of the Passover, and just like they sanctified it when they asked Pilate to crucify Jesus Christ and deliver Barabbas (Matt. 27:15-25; John 18:38-40). The Lord declares that He considers the punishment of the wicked as a sacrifice; and these people think they honor Him by leaving the wicked unpunished and by refusing to see justice done.

THE PUNISHMENT OF GOD AGAINST THOSE WHO SHOW MERCY TO THE WICKED AGAINST HIS WILL, AND UPON THOSE WHO WERE NOT PUNISHED BY ORDINARY JUSTICE ACCORDING TO THEIR DEEDS; AND THOSE WHO TOLERATE THE GUILTY AND CAUSE THE INNOCENT TO BE KILLED

TIMOTHY: I have seen many to whom mercy has been shown, who truly rendered to the rulers who favored them the payment they deserved.

DANIEL: You have a good example of this in Ahab. He showed mercy to Ben-hadad the king of Syria, whom God delivered into his hands in order to bring him to justice. And because Ahab did not execute justice against him, the prophet of God declared to him that Ahab would take the place of the man he had let escape, and that he would pay with his own life, and that this same man would be his executioner—as it truly happened, for Ahab was killed in the war against the Syrians, which war would not have been fought against him if he had punished their king as he deserved, instead of entering into a treaty with him (1 Kings 20:30-43).

David was indeed a very different man than Ahab, and had a much greater reason to show mercy to Absalom his son who had killed his own brother Amnon, than Ahab ever had to do the same for Ben-hadad. But yet his own son to whom he showed grace was one of the most horrible scourges he ever felt in his life. For he did not rest until he had chased his own father from his kingdom, and until he had ruined all (2 Sam. 15:10-14). And though he was not punished by his father for the murder he treacherously committed against his own brother, nevertheless he was slain by the hand of God, who well knew how to find other means to work His vengeance and justice upon him. For, as he had been the executioner of his own brother out of vengeance for the wrong he had done to his sister Tamar in violating her, so also God placed him in the hands of Joab, who killed him, having found him hanging from a tree, who could not be delivered from death even by the authority and command of his own father, though he was the king, as we already discussed previously (2 Sam. 13:1-20; 18:10-15). For when God wills to execute justice, there is no power that can hinder Him. And if those who have a command from Him to execute it do not carry out their orders as their office requires, God indeed will not fail to see it done by one means or another, and He will find servants to carry it out.

Saul did not execute his charge against Agag the king of the Amalekites, but that king did not in any way escape execution, and did not remain unpunished for his sins (1 Sam. 15:7-9, 20-33). Likewise Ahab tolerated and supported the false prophets of Baal, but God executed justice against them by means of Elijah (1 Kings 18:1-40).

TIMOTHY: It happened to these two kings as it does to modern-day tyrants who persecute the Church of the Lord. They spared and supported the guilty, as appears in these examples, and on the other hand they persecuted the innocent to death, as we have already shown in the example of the death of the priests of Nob who were killed by the command of Saul and in the example of Naboth who was killed by the command of Ahab (1 Sam. 22:18-19; 1 Kings 21:7-13). In the same way the vast majority of kings and rulers today show clemency to the wickedest men of the world, and tolerate blasphemers, idolaters, Epicureans, atheists, adulterers, heretics, thieves, Sodomites, and other such abominable criminals, and yet they put to death the poor sheep of Jesus Christ.

DANIEL: It is true.

CHAPTER EIGHT

Killing in Self-Defense: Is It Murder?

THOSE WHO KILL A MAN IN SELF-DEFENSE; AND OF THE LAW WHICH ALLOWS US TO REPEL VIOLENCE WITH VIOLENCE

TIMOTHY: Yet these examples you quoted clearly declare that God wills that the sentence He has given against willful murderers be executed without any tolerance and regard to persons, which, in my opinion, we must also understand of all other evil deeds worthy of death. But we have not yet finished the matter of those who kill in self defense.

DANIEL: It is true that the civil laws grant permission to repel violence by violence, and that they set forth this law as a natural law necessary for the preservation of humankind. If the magistrate, who is the minister of God (Rom. 13:4), has by law permitted the attacked to use force against his aggressor, and to take away his life if the aggressor seeks to kill him, we can respond to this that the attacked individual repels the violence of the aggressor not as a private individual, but as a public officer, being armed with the authority and sword of the magistrate against lawbreakers who seek to disturb the public peace and violate the civil society of mankind.

And what you say of him who is attacked in his own person must also be understood of those who defend others who are joined to them and who are under their care, such as husbands of their wives, and fathers and mothers of their children. For these are not only constrained by necessity (as if the violence were done against their own persons), but are also constrained by their responsibility and office.

For, firstly, when a man (or one of his own) is in such danger, there is no time to appeal to the magistrate for assistance. Therefore if he desires to await his aid to be delivered from this danger and to repulse the wrong done to him, he will perish before the assistance arrives.

Secondly, if he who is attacked has no more rights than the aggressor, the aggressors would take much greater boldness, and good men would live in much greater danger than the wicked. This is the point from which it seems to me that this law draws its foundation in the Word of God, added to the fact that the Law of God gave to the Israelites some similarity with this in the law given against thieves at night and those who break into houses (Ex. 22:1-2). Therefore the equity in the one case can also be taken in some way in the other. But yet, seeing that we do not have an express law of God by which He clearly gives us such authority, and seeing that it is more dangerous to abuse this privilege than anything else, the best and surest method, if it be possible, is to live in such a way that we have no need of this law [Rom. 12:18].

WHETHER A MAN WHO KILLS SOMEONE IN DEFENSE OF HIS LIFE OR OF SOMEONE ELSE'S REMAINS INNOCENT OF MURDER BEFORE GOD

TIMOTHY: And if it is not possible to avoid such an occurrence, what should we do? Must we permit the murderer to kill us and our wives and children?

DANIEL: If such a case befalls us, we must not think that we are wholly blameless before God (though we are in the eyes of human justice), particularly if we have acted in any way out of a spirit of revenge. For human justice often allows many things for the preservation of public peace which are however very far from the perfection of Christians. But it does this in part because of the hardness and wickedness of human hearts, out of a similar consideration as divorce was permitted to the Jews by Moses (Matt. 19:7-8), in part because it is difficult to remove in any other way many of the other evils which are daily committed. It is indeed difficult for a man to kill another out of self-defense—no matter how good a cause he might have—without mixing with it anger and wrath unworthy of a Christian man.

Therefore whoever has killed, no matter how innocent he is before men, he is always considered a manslayer before God if any evil affection on his part was mingled with the deed, until he has obtained pardon from Him. And in order that this privilege which is given to the attacked might not give them too much boldness and not enough fear of killing their aggressors and of staining their hands in the blood of their brothers, it is truly necessary that those who have killed be not lightly declared innocent before there is firstly a fair inquiry made into the innocence, blamelessness, and justice of the attacked. For many who kill because they were assaulted have often provoked the aggressor to attack them. When it is so, it is always good for the manslayer to understand, no matter how just a cause he might have, that he is not praised for having killed, and that he has escaped more by grace than by his merit. And he ought to consider it a great judgment of God upon him that he has been placed in such an unpleasant situation, if he was not called by God to this by some special and extraordinary calling, as Moses was when he killed the Egyptian in order to defend the Hebrew from the man's violent assault, just as Stephen declares (Ex. 2:11-12; Acts 7:23-25).

For if he who killed his neighbor by accident had a just reason to be grieved and displeased with himself (though it was stated in the Law that God delivered into his hand the man who was killed), how much more must he be who has killed his enemy by such an unpleasant occurrence, and who in this way has acted as an executioner of his brother? I say this even of those very ones who in such a case have the best cause in the world. For if he who did the deed was driven by any desire for revenge, he did not have so just a cause as the executioner who does what he does by the command of justice, and as the magistrate commanded to do this by the command that God placed him under.

THE SLAUGHTER OF BEASTS, AND IN WHAT WAYS IT IS PERMITTED OR FORBIDDEN BY GOD, AND THE HUMANITY REQUIRED TOWARD THEM

TIMOTHY: I am quite content with the conclusion you have given me on this point. I now willingly ask your opinion of the belief both of those who forbid and create difficulties in the slaughter of beasts, as well as those who consider it unlawful for a Christian man to kill any man at all, no matter the reason, not even by magistrates themselves who have been publicly commanded by God to do so; but who declare that we must patiently endure all that the wicked do because the Law says "Thou shalt not kill," and because Jesus Christ forbade the resistance of evil and commanded us not to render evil for evil.

It seems to me that the first have no foundation at all, seeing that this law was not given for beasts, but for men, and that God has given the beasts to us as meat (Gen. 1:28-30; 9:3; Deut. 14:4-6, 9, 11). The second, in my opinion, has scarcely any better foundation, if I have properly understood what you said concerning the office of the magistrate: to punish the evildoers and to execute the commandments they have received from God.

DANIEL: This permission which God gave man, which you just mentioned, clearly declares that we must not understand this law to speak of the slaughtering of beasts, but of the killing of men. For we can indeed employ the flesh of beasts as meat without being guilty of murdering them. And if it is lawful to kill domesticated animals and livestock from whom we receive no harm, but rather great profit, we have much greater reason to kill the savage and venomous beasts and those which are a danger to men. Therefore we can leave these reveries to the Pythagoreans, Manicheans, and other similar dreamers and heretics who follow them, who abstain from eating flesh out of a fear of finding the soul of their fathers and mothers in the beasts they have killed, because of the belief they hold of the transmigration of souls from one body to another.

Yet there is one point on this matter which it is useful for us to consider. Though God has subjected the beasts to us and has allowed us to use them, yet He admonishes us not to be cruel to them, in order that by showing ourselves humane to them, we might show ourselves more so to men who are our own flesh and blood; as we already mentioned when we discussed the prohibition against eating blood, and likewise in the commandment of the Day of Rest concerning beasts, in which we also discussed how the Lord willed to instruct us in this humaneness by the Law in which He forbade taking the mother of the young birds in the nest with her little ones (Deut. 22:6-7).

Solomon gives us a clear declaration of these things when he says: "A righteous man regardeth the life of his beast: but the tender mercies of the wicked are cruel" (Prov. 12:10)—that is, a just man is humane even to his beasts, and cares for and protects them while he uses them. The wicked does not do so, but is of a cruel nature, devoid of humanity, who exacts of his beast as much as he can without killing it, and more than it can bear, in such a way that it often seems to live under its burdens. This happens particularly in many cruel men when they employ hired beasts, which they force to labor more than they are able, and also treat them cruelly. This is why it is also written in Ecclesiasticus: "Have you cattle? Take care of them, and if they bring you profit, keep them."[1] It is also written in the Law: "Thou shalt not muzzle the ox when he treadeth out the corn" (Deut. 24:5; 1 Cor. 9:9; 1 Tim. 5:18).

TIMOTHY: There is yet still another manner by which we offend God by killing beasts—that is, when we kill another man's beast, to the harm of our neighbors. But this manner pertains more to the commandment given against stealing and to the others which concern the goods of our neighbors rather than to this commandment which concerns their persons.

DANIEL: It is true. God also gave laws on this concerning the beasts which kill others, and concerning the thieves who kill the beasts they steal, by which laws we can understand how a man is to be judged in such a case.

[1] Ecclesiasticus 7:22. Though Viret cites the Apocrypha, he did not believe these writings to be inspired, but merely employed them for their historical value, just as he quotes Josephus, Aristotle, and others.

CHAPTER NINE

Magistrates and the Death Penalty

THOSE WHO CONSIDER THAT IT IS NOT LAWFUL FOR A CHRISTIAN TO EXERCISE THE OFFICE OF A MAGISTRATE OR TO SENTENCE AN EVILDOER TO DEATH; AND THE CHARGE AND POWER GIVEN BY GOD TO MAGISTRATES IN SUCH A CASE; AND THE LAWS HE GAVE THEM TO LEAD AND GUIDE THEM IN THIS

TIMOTHY: You have not yet responded to those who are of the belief that it is not lawful—not even for magistrates themselves—to punish evildoers, and who conclude from this that no Christian can be a magistrate.

DANIEL: There are none who do not clearly understand that by this they wholly and openly contravene all the laws of God, who commands us to punish the transgressors of these commandments, be it by death or some other penalty according to what they deserve, whether they have transgressed the commandments of the first or the second table, as appears by these laws: "He that sacrificeth unto any god, save unto the LORD only, he shall be utterly destroyed" (Ex. 22:20); "And the soul that turneth after such as have familiar spirits, and after wizards, to go a whoring after them, I will even set My face against that soul, and will cut him off from among his people" (Lev. 20:6; Deut. 13:1-5). The same is also commanded of blasphemers: "And he that blasphemeth the name of the Lord, he shall surely be put to death, and all the congregation shall certainly stone him: as well the stranger, as he that is born in the land, when he blasphemeth the name of the Lord, shall be put to death" (Lev. 24:16).

TIMOTHY: All these laws were given for the preservation of the commandments of the first table.

DANIEL: The Lord has done the same for the second table. For we have the laws which were given against children who rebel against their parents, and against adulterers, those who commit incest, Sodomites, those who give false testimony, and murderers and manslayers, who by these laws are all judged and condemned to death (Lev. 20:9-16; 18:6-23; 24:19-22; Deut. 22:22-24). But how can this commandment be truly kept without the law given against murderers? For when the Law commands: "Whoso sheddeth man's blood, by man shall his blood be shed," and: "all they that take the sword shall perish with the sword," it shows us that we are required to shed human blood in order that human blood be not shed, and to kill with the sword in order to prevent killing with the sword (Gen. 9:6; Matt. 26:52). Thus it follows that the magistrate to whom this charge is given is not the enemy of human blood and of human civil society (as are the murderers and criminals), but rather that he is the friend and preserver of it by putting an end to murders and crime.

TIMOTHY: It is true.

DANIEL: This is why Paul wrote to Timothy: "I exhort therefore, that, first of all, supplications, prayers, intercessions, and giving of thanks, be made for all men; for kings, and for all that are in authority; that we may lead a quiet and peaceable life in all godliness and honesty. For this is good and acceptable in the sight of God our Saviour" (1 Tim. 2:1-3). Paul clearly shows us by these words that rulers and magistrates are not ordained by God to trouble and destroy human society, but to preserve it in peace. And therefore he admonishes all the Church and all believers in the person of Timothy, to pray for all those who are in such a position, indeed even for those who are unbelievers, just as Jeremiah exhorted the Jews to pray for the prosperity of Babylon which was at that time the ruler of the people, and particularly of the Israelites who were exiles in her, saying: "seek the peace of the city whither I have caused you to be carried away captives, and pray unto the LORD for it: for in the peace thereof shall ye have peace" (Jer. 29:7).

On this we must note two points.

The first is that the Lord makes even tyrants and unbelievers serve for the good of His Church and for the peace of His own, according to His good pleasure.

The other is that He supports and favors them because of His Church, and He is pleased when the Church prays for her magistrates, whoever they may be, whether believers or unbelievers, tyrants or good rulers (as Paul also declared), and that the believers' prayers will greatly benefit them.

Seeing that it is true that this office is ordained for such a good end, and that by it God makes even His enemies serve for the good of His people, why would believers and His true servants not also serve in this office and in a work so holy and just? And if we are commanded to pray for tyrants themselves and for unbelieving magistrates (as also the Church of old has always done when she was subjected to them), how much more ought we to pray for good rulers and believing magistrates?

TIMOTHY: It is easy to perceive.

THE ERROR OF THE ANABAPTISTS AND THOSE LIKE THEM WHO SEEK TO ABOLISH CHRISTIAN MAGISTRATES, AND THE REASON FOR THIS; AND HOW THE MAGISTRATE IS THE

HAND OF GOD IN THE EXECUTIONS HE CARRIES OUT BY HIS COMMANDMENT

DANIEL: Therefore I am astonished at the Anabaptists who have arisen in our times, and who adhere to this belief (though all those who are considered to be of this sect do not hold to this opinion, as they have truly declared by their works).

TIMOTHY: That is certainly the truth. For those who have taken the sword into their own hands in an attempt to raise themselves up against the magistrates and civil powers, and who have incited the people to revolt and rebel against their lords, have certainly turned to the other extreme.

DANIEL: The number of them has not been small. All this error proceeds from a lack of understanding of what this office of rulers and magistrates is, and the difference which must be placed between personal revenge committed by a man's own authority and passion, and the public justice which is carried out according to the command and authority of God by the sword He placed in the hands of the magistrate. For, as Paul said: "he beareth not the sword in vain," or "without cause" (Rom. 13:4). Therefore when the magistrate executes someone he is commanded by God to execute, he does not do this on his own authority apart from the calling of God, but it is God who executes him by the hand of this man, according to the power lawfully ordained by Him. For, though none can be executed and put to death without the will and permission of God, yet there is a vast difference between the work of him who does what he does by the commandment of God, having regard for His will and for the calling to which he has been called, and the work of him who has no commandment and serves no one but his own passions, without having any regard either for the will of God or for the legitimate calling He has established.

Thus the magistrate puts to death, not to satisfy his own pleasure or revenge (if he is a just magistrate), nor to multiply murders, but to hinder and abolish them. And if he does not do so and does not execute those who deserve it, he will be executed by God Himself instead of those he ought to have executed, as we mentioned previously. And when he performs all things according to his charge, he does not simply kill the man whom God has forbidden from killing, but he will also kill the criminal, adulterer, blasphemer, and evildoer whom God has commanded to be put to death by the laws He gave as explanations and expositions of the one He gave in this commandment.

TIMOTHY: Those who hold to this error will truly agree with you, but they say that it was lawful to do so in the Old Testament, and that unbelieving magistrates can still do so, but they declare that this is not lawful for Christians, seeing that Jesus Christ has forbidden all vengeance.

DANIEL: You have already heard what we discussed on this head concerning personal and public vengeance, and concerning that which is done by the commandment of God and that which is done out of personal passion. To this we could still add that it is helpful to consider the difference between the political, spiritual, civil, and ecclesiastical jurisdictions. For one does not abolish the other, and they are not contrary to each other, but rather they assist each other. For if God commanded that punishment be executed against those who transgress the Law, and that the vengeance He has reserved to Himself be carried out, who can more justly do this than Christian magistrates who are by their position ordained to be preservers of the Law of the Lord? What more just and loyal officers could He have?

But out of a lack of considering this well, and the difference which the Lord has placed between the political, spiritual, civil, and ecclesiastical administration, the Anabaptists have fallen into these errors and frenzies. They act as though the Gospel was proclaimed in order to confound all order and mix temporal and spiritual administrations all together, and abolish one by the other. Thus the Christian man must not have any difficulty in exercising the office of a magistrate if he is called to it by God, but to the contrary he must only guard himself against abusing it.

HOW RULERS AND MAGISTRATES CAN BE MURDERERS NOT ONLY BY KILLING THE INNOCENT, BUT ALSO THE GUILTY; AND THE END TO WHICH THEY MUST LOOK IN THIS

TIMOTHY: You have touched upon a point which rulers and magistrates must heed well. For, though God has given them power over the life of men, yet if they wrongly put someone to death, they are no less murderers and manslayers than other men.

DANIEL: Indeed, they are even more so, and are worthy of a much more grievous judgment before God because they have, under His title whose name they bear, condemned those whom their sovereign Ruler has declared innocent, and have released those whom He has condemned; disguising their crimes under the name and veil of justice, just as Ahab did in the death of righteous Naboth, in order to possess his vineyard by confiscation. For this he and his Jezebel, who counseled him on the means of doing it, received the reward they merited (1 Kings 21:1-25). For such rulers and magistrates are true public criminals, and are ministers of the devil, and not of God.

TIMOTHY: Truly the most dangerous and the most horrible crime that can exist in the world is that which is disguised under the mantle of justice.

DANIEL: There is still one further way by which those who hold the sword of God can commit homicides and murders. For the officer of justice is not only a murderer when he puts the innocent to death, but also when he puts to death the guilty who deserve death, if he does it not out of a zeal and desire he has for justice or for the glory of God and the preservation of the public peace (having regard for his calling and office), but either out of enmity, malevolence, revenge, or greed, and the worldly profit which he might accrue by it either by confiscations or by some other means. For when a magistrate punishes lawbreakers, he must do so as a father who, because of the wickedness of his son, is constrained to chastise him, yet does so with great regret, following God's example, who much prefers the conversion and life of poor sinners than their damnation and death, and who is greatly moved when He is constrained to prosecute them.

TIMOTHY: There are many who do not give this much thought at all. For there are some who take less thought over the death of a man than they do over that of a calf or a kid. And there are others who never bring anyone to justice unless they seek to be avenged upon them—unless they are truly constrained to do it.

DANIEL: I have often seen by experience what you say. There are others who are indeed quite joyous when their poor subjects fall into some error from which they can collect some fine, and who never punish or bring anyone to justice unless by doing so they receive some benefit or can line their pockets from it.

TIMOTHY: I am well acquainted with many such as these.

THE REASONS WHY GOD COMMANDED MAGISTRATES TO EXECUTE PENALTIES AND PUNISHMENTS PUBLICLY

DANIEL: Although such people abuse their office in one way or another, they truly err more grievously by leaving the wicked unpunished than by punishing the guilty without doing it with the proper regard for justice which they ought to have. For God did not command without many just and righteous reasons that the wicked are to be punished by the magistrates.

In the first place, He wills to declare by these officers (who represent His image in executing justice) that there is a God who hates iniquity and who places a difference between good and evil and between justice and injustice.

Secondly, seeing that He is the Preserver of mankind, He also desires to make us understand that He is the Preserver of the political order, and that He wills that all who trouble it (and human society likewise) be removed and separated from it by the sword of the magistrate, which is universally ordained against all these, as a common necessity.

Therefore we see by experience that God by His providence delivers into the hands of the magistrates even those who escaped from them, in order that they might be punished by them. Besides this, these punishments also serve as examples to others, in order that the fear of the punishment which they see the wicked undergo might restrain them from evil-doing, and might warn them to at least keep themselves free from external works which disturb the public society of men.

These examples are also set forth by the commandment of God to warn us (by the punishments of those we see punished by His commandment) of the much more terrifying judgment which is prepared for all those who do not within this world seek and obtain remission of their sins by the Son of God alone, the sole Mediator between God and men, and the Judge of the living and the dead.

CHAPTER TEN

Just and Unjust Wars

WAR, AND UNDER WHAT CONDITIONS IT IS LAWFUL OR UNLAWFUL FOR CHRISTIANS TO ENGAGE IN IT

TIMOTHY: All that you have said concerning these matters is a great help to me, in my opinion, for the better understanding of two points which I must still ask you about. The first concerns wars, and the other concerns courts and legal proceedings. For I conclude from what you have said that, because the magistrate "bears the sword" of God for the defense of the good and "to execute wrath upon him that doeth evil" by order of the justice commanded by God (Rom. 13:4), he is also appointed to do the same in a just war, when he is battling a foe who, trampling upon justice and reason, resorts to force and violence.

DANIEL: If it is lawful for a magistrate to punish a small group of evildoers by a small number of his subjects and officers, it is no less lawful for him to punish a great multitude of evildoers by a vast number of his subjects when necessity constrains him to do so. But a ruler must with all diligence carefully consider the matter before undertaking a war, and seek every means possible to avoid it and to restore peace, considering the great and horrible evils which generally accompany war, in order that the medicine might not be worse than the disease which he desires to cure by it.

TIMOTHY: From what I can understand, all war is evil inasmuch as it can never occur without great iniquity and vast injustice either on one side or the other. If the injustice exists on both sides, it is so much the worse. But it is good as far as it is founded upon right and justice, in order to preserve the honor of God and the Church and the public good, and to set to rights unbearable evils, and inasmuch as God by His just judgment uses such scourges to chastise the iniquities of men.

DANIEL: You speak well. Thus it follows that rulers and magistrates who wage war without a regard for these things, but who instead look only to their own ambition, vengeance, greed, rapacity, and tyranny, are true public criminals, and the head chiefs and captains of other criminals.

UNDER WHAT TITLE AND UNDER WHAT CONDITIONS THE SUBJECTS OF RULERS CAN JUSTLY ENGAGE IN THE WARS WAGED BY THEIR RULERS

TIMOTHY: If these are chiefs and captains of criminals, those who battle under them cannot be guiltless of the same crime.

DANIEL: There are two things to consider on this. The first is that the subject can be ignorant of the true cause of the war and the justness or unjustness of it, just as Joab was ignorant of the reason why David commanded him to have Uriah killed. For, not knowing why David ordered it done, he could assume that he certainly had a just reason for doing so, and that his duty was only to obey the commandment of his ruler.

The other thing which we must still consider is that a subject does not have the authority to demand a reason from his ruler for what he commands and what he does. For what order could exist if a ruler were required to give all his officers and subjects a reason for everything he commanded them to do? The subject thus can do nothing but obey the commandment of his ruler when he cannot be a judge of the cause, except in a case when he so clearly recognizes the iniquity that he cannot fulfill his command without clearly violating his own conscience. For a man is not required to kill all those whom his ruler commands him to kill simply because of the whim of his ruler. What if your ruler commanded you to kill a righteous man in order that he could ravish his wife? Or what if he required you to persecute and kill the faithful who follow the Word of God? Ought you to obey him?

TIMOTHY: I do not think so. For I cannot believe that God approved of the deeds of the inhabitants of the city of Naboth when they put that righteous man to death to satisfy the will and commandment of Queen Jezebel (1 Kings 21:11-14).

But if I was under the rule of a tyrant and refused to do what he commanded me, I would place my goods and my life in grave danger.

DANIEL: It is much better to lose both body and goods than to offend God and lose your soul along with your life and earthly possessions. For in such a case we must always cling to the rule of the apostles: "We ought to obey God rather than men," and to what Jesus Christ said: "Rather fear him which is able to destroy both soul and body in hell" (Acts 5:29; Matt. 10:28).

THOSE WHO ENGAGE IN WARS MERELY FOR THEIR OWN PLEASURE, OR TO OBTAIN GOLD OR TO PILLAGE

TIMOTHY: We have spoken of subjects and their role in wartime, but what must we say of those who, without being subjects or constrained to go to war either by duty toward their ruler or by some just alliance or good cause, willingly engage in wars and happily become executioners simply to obtain gold or to pillage and plunder, without having any regard either for right or justice, but only for their own greed and thirst for ill-gotten gains?

DANIEL: It is easy to judge. For who can excuse these men of homicide, murder, and criminal activities before God, seeing that they do not do what they do by His command or with a regard for His will, but only for their own profit and to satisfy their own desires? (1 Tim. 6:10.)

TIMOTHY: If this is true, it can then happen that a soldier engaged in an unjust war—that is, unjust concerning the ruler who leads him—can yet be innocent on his part; and another, being engaged in a just war with regards to his ruler, could be guilty on his part. For if he who engages in a just war goes to war without a lawful calling and without regard for justice, but only with a concern for what we have just said, there is no doubt that he would be guilty, instead of the other who was engaged in an unjust war but only went out of obedience to his magistrate, and not knowing that the cause was unjust, would be innocent.

DANIEL: It is true.

THE USE OF THE MAGISTRATE IN LEGAL PROCEEDINGS, AND UNDER WHAT CONDITIONS AND FOR WHAT PURPOSE CHRISTIANS CAN GO TO COURT AND HAVE RECOURSE TO THE MAGISTRATES TO PROTECT THEIR RIGHTS

TIMOTHY: In my opinion, what we have said of wars also opens the question of what needs to be said concerning legal proceedings.

DANIEL: It is certain that if we have recourse to a magistrate only to maintain our right, without a desire to injure our adversaries in any way, and without bearing them any hatred and enmity, we can make use of the order ordained by God for this end, as a good creation of His, created for our use and for our good. For if the thing were not good in itself, God would not have ordained it. But we must beware of abusing it, just as the other good creatures and ordinances of God. For, no matter how just a cause we might have, if we bear some speck of hatred, enmity, and a thirst for revenge and injury against our adversaries, we wickedly abuse the ordinance of God, which was not given for the purpose of ruining our neighbor, but for his edification, neither to seek out our own personal revenge, but rather the vengeance of God. And, because it is more difficult than anything else to have a lawsuit without enmity and without a thirst for revenge, we must, as much as is possible for us, follow the counsel of Jesus Christ and of Paul which we already previously mentioned in this matter (Matt. 5:25-26; 1 Cor. 6:6-8).

And if we pursue someone in justice, we must do it not only out of a defense for our own right, but also with a concern for restraining the evildoers, by the authority of God, for the preservation of the public peace; and for removing the liberty that they might take of doing evil if they were always to remain unpunished. If we have a regard for any other thing, and if we take pleasure in the evil that befalls our neighbor because of the enmity we bear them, we are murderers just as much as the judge who punishes the evildoer worthy of punishment not out of any desire he has for justice, but out of his enmity and his own thirst for revenge. Thus we must employ this remedy as a medicine in which it is useful to remember two things. The first is that we must not use it without a just need. The other, that when we are constrained to use it, we must always begin by the easiest, lightest, and most merciful remedies, without proceeding to extremes unless we are constrained to do so by the wickedness of our adversaries.

CHAPTER ELEVEN

Self-Murder and Suicide

THOSE WHO KILL THEMSELVES, AND THE REASONS WHY THIS IS NOT LAWFUL, AND FROM WHERE SUCH MURDERS AND MANSLAUGHTERS PROCEED

TIMOTHY: It seems to me that we have dealt quite fully and sufficiently with the matters pertaining to this commandment. Nothing now remains except one point on which I do not have much difficulty. For, if it is not lawful for a man to kill another man, I do not think that it can be lawful for him to kill himself.

DANIEL: It is true that a man ought to have more authority over his own deeds than over those of another man, and over his own body than over that of another. But, seeing that man did not enter this world by his own power, but to the contrary was placed here by God, so it is not lawful for him to leave this world without the permission of Him who placed him here, nor by any other means than those which He Himself has ordained for him. Therefore if God has threatened vengeance upon those who take away the life of others by some other means than those which He has ordained, we must not doubt that He will count it an even greater sin for those who work such violence upon themselves; for such an act clearly declares a great impatience and an abysmal despair, unless the act happened by some malady in which the man was transported out of his right mind. For in such a case I could not rashly condemn all those who kill themselves by such an accident, though such cases are witnesses of the grave judgments of God, by which it seems that He in His wrath hands the reins to Satan, to drive such poor miserable men into such temptations and such madness.

For, seeing that life is such an excellent gift of God, and that He has placed a natural love and desire for it not only in all men, but also in all the other creatures—indeed, so great that there is none comparable to it—and that He has in all manners forbidden killing and the shedding of human blood except by the conditions and exceptions that we discussed concerning this, it is absolutely certain that this desire for death which induces men to commit self-murder and destroy themselves either by an impatience proceeding from fear, pain, despair, or by some other similar cause, proceeds from the devil and not from God; as we can judge by the swine who cast themselves into the sea after Jesus Christ gave permission to the devils to enter them, which they would never have done by themselves (Matt. 8:30-32).

TIMOTHY: Then you do not share the opinion of the ancient pagans, who often considered the death of those who killed themselves to be a great glory, believing that this proceeded from a deep inward power and fortitude.

DANIEL: This deep power and fortitude was no more than a vain glory and a deep pride and haughtiness of courage, and a desperate impatience, which was the reason why they could not patiently bear the disgrace and afflictions that God brought upon them. I speak this even of those who were the most virtuous and honorable among them. Therefore I cannot approve as an act worthy of a true servant of God, of what is written in the second book of Maccabees concerning the death of a certain Razis, who killed himself (as the history says) so that he might not fall into the hands of his enemies.[1]

[1] 2 Maccabees 14:37-46.

For this is a deed which better resembles the pagans than the true servants of God who were led and guided by His Spirit. For, if it pleased God to deliver them into the hands of their enemies, they much preferred their enemies to be their executioners rather than they themselves.

We truly read that Saul, the first king of Israel, was his own executioner, as were also Ahithophel and Judas (1 Sam. 31:2-5; 2 Sam. 17:23; Matt. 27:3-5). But we never read such examples of the true servants of God. Indeed, we read that they were often tempted to kill themselves, as Job himself testifies, saying: "My soul chooseth strangling, and death rather than my life" (Job 7:15). But he did not proceed as far as the act, nor did he fall into such despair as Satan wished to gain over him, seeing that God did not allow him to proceed that far, but instead forbade him from touching either his soul or his life (Job 1:11; 2:6).

TIMOTHY: The example of Samson could be brought forth, who killed himself, and yet he was a servant of God and was led by His Spirit, who gave him power even in that very moment to do what he did (Judges 16:28-30).

DANIEL: But you see clearly in the historical account that Samson was not like those of whom we just spoke, but was instead a valiant man and a brave and courageous captain who voluntarily risked his life to defeat his enemies and avenge the injury done by them against God and His people.

BRIEF CONCLUSION OF THE MATTERS CONTAINED IN THIS COMMANDMENT AND IN THIS CONVERSATION

TIMOTHY: I am now satisfied on all the questions I had concerning this commandment. Therefore, in conclusion, in order to rightly keep this commandment, we must not only beware of keeping our hands, tongues, and hearts from all enmity and from all ways and signs of it, but we must also patiently bear all the wrongs done to us, and we must endeavor to do to our brethren—be they friends or enemies—all the good that we can, contrary to the evil which is forbidden us, exercising all love toward them.

DANIEL: This is indeed the purpose of this commandment, under which we can summarize all the matters contained in it. Now it only remains for us to beware of a great evil to which all men are subject—and yet, despite this evil, they live in assurance as if they had nothing to fear, for they do not think of it and do not consider it as they ought to.

TIMOTHY: What evil is this?

DANIEL: It is that true murderers or manslayers before God are those who murder by deed and by hand, or even by word or by heart and will, or by an envy and hatred that we bear to each other, or in desiring and wishing another's evil and death. And the less that we think of this and the less that we consider the wrong, so much the greater is our danger.

CHAPTER TWELVE

Innocent Blood and the Defilement of a Land

A Sermon by John Calvin

If one be found slain in the land which the LORD thy God giveth thee to possess it, lying in the field, and it be not known who hath slain him: then thy elders and thy judges shall come forth, and they shall measure unto the cities which are round about him that is slain: and it shall be, that the city which is next unto the slain man, even the elders of that city shall take an heifer, which hath not been wrought with, and which hath not drawn in the yoke; and the elders of that city shall bring down the heifer unto a rough valley, which is neither eared nor sown, and shall strike off the heifer's neck there in the valley: and the priests the sons of Levi shall come near; for them the LORD thy God hath chosen to minister unto Him, and to bless in the name of the LORD; and by their word shall every controversy and every stroke be tried: and all the elders of that city, that are next unto the slain man, shall wash their hands over the heifer that is beheaded in the valley: and they shall answer and say, Our hands have not shed this blood, neither have our eyes seen it. Be merciful, O LORD, unto Thy people Israel, whom Thou hast redeemed, and lay not innocent blood unto Thy people of Israel's charge. And the blood shall be forgiven them. So shalt thou put away the guilt of innocent blood from among you, when thou shalt do that which is right in the sight of the LORD.

— Deuteronomy 21:1-9

I have spoken of this law already, and have briefly declared what God meant by ordaining this ceremony: namely, that we should abhor the shedding of blood, and murders, and violence. He spoke previously of the law of arms. And now He adds that the killing of even one man is a defiling of the entire country unless the remedy is sought by praying to God to forgive the fault, and by solemnly declaring that none of the inhabitants of that land are guilty of it. We see then that men's lives are precious to God since He wills to have so solemn a redress be made for a murder committed—indeed, even when the perpetrator is unknown and when the truth cannot be found out.

If a man had been murdered and the murderer was known, then this ceremony would not be sufficient, for God commands the crime to be punished. And if a murderer is permitted to escape, the judges and all the people become guilty of the fact.

But when it is unknown by whom a man was slain, then God declares that it is not enough for every man to solemnly declare for himself that he was neither party nor privy to the matter; but He also wills that the town where the deed was done (or which was nearest to the place where the deed was done) should be examined for it. For we know that a partition of the towns and villages was made to every tribe. Thus every city had a countryside surrounding it, and the towns and villages in it were called as it were the daughters of that city. Yet despite this, in this case our Lord willed to have them make a new survey and measurement of the distance of the places again, and that the city which was found to be nearest to the dead body should be obliged to make a solemn sacrifice, at which He willed to have the elders, judges, and priests present.

He sets down the priests by name, both for sacrificing and also because it was their duty to make the atonement. Whenever any uncleanness occurred, so as the people were defiled before God, it was the duty of the priests to make them clean again towards God. And that was the reason why that order was required to be present in this case. And therefore Moses adds that: "them the LORD thy God hath chosen to minister unto Him, and to bless in the name of the LORD" (Deut. 21:5), and that it belongs to them to judge leprosies and all other similar things, and all other kinds of uncleanness by which the people might be defiled. In attributing this office to them, he declares what purpose their presence ought to serve in this act.

Also, there was prayer to be made, and the priests were commanded to offer this. And because the whole priestly order was a figure of our Lord Jesus Christ, they blessed in God's name, as I previously declared, and as I shall show somewhat more as I pass over it later. And therefore our Lord appointed them to make the solemn prayer that is set down here.

Now we see what this Law aimed at: namely, that our Lord has showed how precious men's lives are unto Him, in order that we on our part might be the more stirred up to receive Him as our Father. For what an unthankfulness is it if God should have so great and so fatherly a care for us—indeed, for us who are but worthless wretches—and yet, despite this, we do not honor Him as His children ought, nor does He find any obedience at our hands? So then, as much as we see our Lord condescending to have a regard for our life, let us be all the more moved to honor Him and to yield Him all reverence.

Here also by this we are shown that we must support our neighbors as much as lies within our power, and we must abstain from all violence. For if murder is so hateful to God that, even though the murderer is unknown, yet a solemn cleansing was required to be made, what will become of us if we spare not our neighbors? Isn't this a setting of ourselves utterly against God? Here then is a bridle to restrain us from all violence and aggression, for unless we desire to be hateful to our God, we must live in peace and brotherly love with all our neighbors. Now I have told you before that, though murder is forbidden us, it is not meant by this that we should only restrain ourselves from drawing our swords to slay men, but also that (because all those who hate their brethren even in secret are murderers) we must beware and see to it that our hearts remain as clean as our hands, and that we abstain from all hatred and enmity. Thus you see what we have to remember in the second place of this Law which is set down here.

For it is not enough for us to love our neighbors and not to have committed any injury or violence against them; but we must also (to the uttermost of our power) be a hindrance that restrains the injury that is done to others. Indeed, it is a great thing to be peaceable, but God requires yet more of His children than that—namely, that they should seek peace towards others. Therefore whenever any man begins quarreling or attempts to wrong his neighbor, we must seek to set ourselves against him as much as we can. I know that every man is not armed with the sword; neither may every one of us take upon himself the authority to redress wrongs, but yet let us have an eye to that which God permits, as far as our duty will allow, and as occasion offers. And by this we will show ourselves not to consent to any injustice, but rather that we are willing to aid and assist the innocent who are oppressed and wronged, whom we must seek to help to the best of our power and ability. That is the third point which we must draw from this text.

THE DUTIES OF JUDGES AND MAGISTRATES

Moreover, let us note that judges and ministers of justice are warned here to do their duties. For it is not enough for them to declare that they have not condoned or favored any evil. Neither is it enough for them to be able to say that they have dealt justly with every man who brought a complaint to them.

But they must also search diligently for wrongdoers, and even if no man speaks to them or persuades them, yet they must of their own selves be vigilant in making inquiry. And if they find any fault committed, they themselves must follow the prosecution of it.

But this is ill-heeded by most judges. For they think that they have attained to the full perfection of virtue and that they are greatly to be commended when they have not refused to give men a hearing. If a man who is wronged comes to lay his case before them, and they hear him and seek to help him, they think that they have acquitted themselves very well. But our Lord is not content with that. For even if the wronged party which received the injury holds his peace and patiently endures the wrong done to him, yet even so the judge or the magistrate who is in office must not refrain from doing his duty just because of that. And therefore it is a foolish and weak argument to say: "We knew nothing of it. No man complained of it." True, but yet the evil was committed, and God sees it, and He has commanded that it must be punished. He wills that all wrongdoing be redressed, and that no liberty be given to the stronger to bear down the weaker. And shall the judge in the meanwhile hold his peace?

Let us mark then, that God will not have the ministers of justice to wink at men's wrongdoings—no, not even if there is no informer, protector, advocate, attorney, or plaintiff to call them to act. For they are bound to punish crimes even of themselves, even if no man prosecutes any suit in law. And what then ought they to do when men seek their assistance and when the injured party comes sorrowing and declaring his grief? If the magistrate does not hear him, or if he scorns him for his complaining or leaves him alone, or perhaps the injured man is so vexed that he is forced to abandon his just cause, and in the meanwhile the offender goes unpunished, shall such treachery be excusable before God?

Yet despite this, we often see that if a man who has

been wronged comes to demand justice, he shall be led on. Indeed, he will not be driven away with a cudgel. No one will tell him that he is only wasting his time, but he will be so driven off with evasions and delays that the poor soul will soon regret that he ever attempted to seek justice, and will be constrained to abandon his rights with untold sorrow. That is the common course which the execution of justice generally takes on the earth.

But we see here that such persons who have so abused their authority will be required to give an account for it. For the heavenly Judge not only desires them to hear men's complaints and to relieve them, but also to make inquiries into wrongdoings and search out matters to the very bottom, even though it is not generally known that any fault has been committed or that any man has been wronged—indeed, even though no man has opened his mouth to complain. And when men have done the best they can, yet the Lord wills that they offer a sacrifice, as if to show that some blame lay upon the country itself until forgiveness of the offenses had been sought.

So then, let us learn on our part that our Lord watches over us in such a way that, though we are oppressed and have all the injuries in the world done to us, yet our Lord does not cease to look after and care for us. True it is (as I said before) that judges and magistrates have here a good lesson, and that they ought to consider that they shall not escape the hands of the Heavenly Judge if they have been negligent in maintaining the justice of good men who have been trodden underfoot. If they do not seek to defend them, they will give a reckoning for that loose, immoral dealing of theirs. For this is exactly the same as if they themselves were in league with the criminals.

GOD'S CARE DISPLAYED IN HIS LAW

From this we must understand that, seeing that God has such

a care of those who are dead, how much more does He behold all of us? Therefore we ought to run boldly to Him for refuge when we pine away in this world, suffering many troubles and afflictions, even though we never speak a word or find any defense or help at all among men, no matter how great our extremity might be. For, though He might not immediately show Himself to be near at hand, yet we mustn't think that He has turned His back upon us, for He takes note of all the wrongs that are done to us. And our tears shall come up before Him (as it is said in the psalm). For David said that the tears of the faithful are stored up as it were in bottles, just as men store up sweet waters in jars and ointments in vials (Ps. 56:8). And so our Lord keeps the tears of those who cry out to Him and who run to Him for refuge. He keeps all those tears of theirs, to be revenged for them at His appointed time.

But we must proceed yet further. For, if God helps those who are dead, this is a sign that we are not like brute beasts. For (as Luke records for us) "He is not a God of the dead, but of the living" (Luke 20:38). Therefore let us conclude that when we are gone out of this world, we will have a better life and will be in the hand of God. See what a record of eternal life is given us in the command that God gives us here—namely, that if a man is found murdered, solemn sacrifice must be made to cleanse the land from the defilement to which it was subject. For by this He declares that after our death we live with Him, and that we must not think that we will be destroyed and come to nothing when God takes us out of this world, but rather that this is but a passage into the second life which He promises us.

Seeing that this was spoken in the Law, we ought to be able to assure ourselves of this today much better than they could. For we have the Holy Scriptures in their entirety. We have the heavenly life revealed to us much more openly in the New Testament than it was veiled to the fathers of old before the coming of our Lord Jesus Christ. And therefore we ought to be so much the more assured of it, and not be like the unbelievers who shudder when they hear death spoken of, as though all were over for them and as though they should utterly perish. But we must understand that, when God gathers us to Him by death, we will not cease to live still for Him. Although a man's body may rot away in corruption like the bodies of brute beasts, yet God is still a faithful keeper of our souls, and they will be preserved in His hand and by His power. By this He gives us hope of the last resurrection, in which we will be wholly restored again. For though we are corruptible now, and tend to corruption by death, we will then be clothed again with such a new nature that the body which is now corruptible and transient will become new and incorruptible when we are renewed after the likeness of our Lord Jesus Christ. Thus you see what we have to remember yet further, in that God shows us the care that He Himself takes of those who are dead.

THE ROLE OF THE PRIESTS

Regarding the things that are here spoken concerning the priests, we needn't spend much time on them. It will be enough to simply speak a word or two about it. Moses said that the priests were ordained to bless in God's name—that is, to offer public prayers (Deut. 21:5). It is true that we today have the same office of offering prayers in the name of the whole church, and that the people must say "Amen," as Paul mentioned in his epistle to the Corinthians (1 Cor. 14:16). But the tribe of Levi and the priests of the Law were particularly called to this office because they were a figure of our Lord Jesus Christ, who is our advocate and our mouth, as it were. Therefore it pertains to our Lord Jesus Christ to offer up our requests to God our Father because they can never be acceptable to God but for His sake. Neither are we worthy to pray to God except as He leads us and makes a way and means for us. Therefore in the time of the Law the priests blessed the people—that is, they made public prayers for them.

Again, here is another thing to notice: the priests' blessing of the people was a witness of God's favor and love for them. And this also pertains to our Lord Jesus Christ, though it doesn't only belong to Him alone, but also to all preachers of the Gospel. When we preach God's mercy, the blessing of God is upon all those who heed us. For it is the same as if God Himself came to declare His favor towards us and that, because we are reconciled to Him, He intends to take us into His keeping.

Seeing then that the doctrine of the Gospel implies such things, we see that all the shepherds of the Christian Church bless the people. But this is not because they are figures of our Lord Jesus Christ, but because of the charge that is committed to them. They do indeed represent His person as His officers; but during the time of the shadows of the ceremonial law, the priests did in some ways stand in the place of our Lord Jesus Christ until His coming. This then was meant by blessing the people in the name of God, as we see that the Lord Jesus Christ Himself demonstrated, for He blessed His disciples by laying His hands upon them (Luke 24:50; Acts 1:4).

Therefore let us run to Him as often as we think upon our own wretchedness. Indeed, because we know that we are worthy to be rejected of God and to be as it were accursed because there is nothing but utter wickedness in us, therefore let us flee to our Lord Jesus Christ. For if God gave to His people under the Law this remedy of being blessed by the priests who were no more than mortal men, shall we fear that our Lord Jesus Christ does not possess sufficient power to cleanse away all our accursedness, so that God shall look favorably upon us and receive us as His children? Then let us heartily give heed to this, and rest upon it with full assurance.

And when we begin to pray, let us assure ourselves that we have an advocate who will make us find favor in His sight. And let us not excuse ourselves as the Papists do, who declare: "I am not worthy to pray to God," but let us be assured that our

Lord Jesus Christ calls us to Him. It is true that we ought to recognize our own unworthiness; yet this ought not to make us wander away when we pray to God or cause us to seek some other support, as those who say: "Such-and-such a saint will be my advocate," or "Such-and-such a saint will be my patroness." Instead of this we must direct ourselves to Him who was given to us by God His father—namely, our Lord Jesus Christ. Thus much concerning the blessing.

Now the worship of God bore with it the sacrifices and all the rest of the ceremonies. And today those who are appointed as ministers of God's Word have the administration of the sacraments because it pertains to God's Word and doctrine, which they declare. But our Lord Jesus is He who made the only and everlasting sacrifice upon which we must rest. And in this we see the foolishness of the Roman Catholics, for the priests believe that they must counterfeit His sacrifice, saying: "Behold, the tribe of Levi was appointed to serve God." Yes, but we must consider what type of sacrifice God requires and allows today. Will He have us slay bulls, sheep, lambs, and other such animals? No indeed. But Paul said that the sacrifices which the shepherds of the Church must offer to God are men's souls, whom they win by the preaching of His word (Rom. 15:16; Phil. 2:17). These they dedicate to God, and that is the worship which He accepts. This is a part of the worship of God which is spiritual. And therefore let us note that we must leave to Jesus Christ alone what the Holy Scripture reserves to Him—namely, the offering up of Himself once for all to purchase for us the everlasting forgiveness of all our sins and to present us clean and pure before God (Acts 13:38-39).

Now then, nothing more remains except this only, that we be confirmed in the power brought to us by His death and passion. And how may this be? By the use of the sacraments. When we receive the Lord's Supper, we do not offer a new sacrifice (as the Papists were accustomed to do in that devilish abomination of their mass). But rather we declare that God is at peace with us when we are grounded in the death and passion of His only Son, and that we are partakers of it. And our receiving of the bread and wine that are given to us is the same as if we were fed with His body and blood as with meat and drink. Thus you see how we ought to apply these things to our instruction which are spoken here concerning the sacrifices that were to be offered to God by the priests of the Law.

CHAPTER THIRTEEN

Cleansing our Hearts and our Hands

Now let us proceed to what Moses adds next. He said that the priests must go with the governors and judges of the city, and "the elders of that city shall take an heifer, . . . and the elders of that city shall bring down the heifer unto a rough valley," or a secret valley, "which is neither eared nor sown, and shall strike off the heifer's neck there in the valley," namely, in a valley that is barren and untilled, like a desert place (Deut. 21:3-4).

This circumstance is set down in order that the bystanders might have a greater fear and terror when they saw the cutting off of the heifer's neck, and because they had come as it were into a secret place. For it is certain that God did not care for the blood of the heifer. "Doth God take care for oxen?" Paul asked (1 Cor. 9:9). His speaking of them is for men's sakes. And therefore let us notice how God pointed out a valley—indeed, even a barren valley—in order that they who were present should conceive a certain terror in themselves. What were they afraid of? Of the cutting off of the heifer's head, as though they said: "Must we come to this desert place, and for such an event?" And what a thing is it when a man who is created in the image of God is slain, and that such a crime should be committed? Will not the sun and moon and all the stars of the sky cry out for vengeance to God? Will not the foundations of the earth draw up an indictment as though it were written on paper or parchment? Thus you see what we must consider by God's appointing such a place for such a circumstance.

Now afterward follows the declaration: "Our hands have not shed this blood, neither have our eyes seen it" (Deut. 21:7). When the judges and governors say: "Our hands have not shed this blood," they mean all of the people as well as themselves. For it is not enough for the rulers themselves to be innocent of the murder, but they speak also in the name and on behalf of the whole body of the people whom they represent. And by this we see that if the magistrates allow any wickedness to lie lurking in any city or country, they themselves are guilty of it, and it is the same before God as if they had given their consent to the doing of the deed. Therefore let men mark this saying well: "Our hands have not shed this blood"—namely, that those who are in authority must answer for the whole body of the people, as far as in them lies. They must see to it that wicked doings are not allowed to settle on the land by their sloth and negligence; but they must search them out diligently and do their duty in this regard. Otherwise it will be in vain for them to say: "I did not shed this blood." No, but you represent the whole people. You were commissioned by God's appointment. Therefore, seeing that you have allowed wickedness to be committed within your jurisdiction, God will require an accounting of it from your hand. And indeed, we see how it is God's will not only in this place but also throughout the whole Holy Scripture, that when any trespass was committed in any tribe, the elders must stand forth as it were to confess the people's offenses in their own persons. For, because they were set in that authority and place of honor, they ought to have known that they would be held to a much stricter and weightier account. That is the point which is to be noted here.

And he adds: "Our eyes have not seen it." And by this

we see (as I said before) that it is not enough for us to have our hands clean, but it is also required that we must not be aware of any evil. For if we conceal our knowledge of it, to whom is it to be imputed? Truly we may well wash our hands of it before men (as Pilate did), as though we should say: "I didn't do it, so I am innocent of it" (Matt. 27:24). But God accepts no such mockery. Therefore whenever we are examined or called to testify about any matter, let us not imagine that we shall escape scot-free before God because we have not done the actual deed. For we must to the uttermost of our power find means to redress the wrong that has been done so that one man might not be trodden underfoot and another be upheld and maintained, and consequently common robbery be allowed to reign disorderly among men; but that right and just dealings may be maintained among men. And let every man further the same on his own behalf.

And, concerning judges and magistrates, let them also learn to have eyes, and let them not turn a blind eye or look the other way when evil is committed. Nor let them think that they will escape if they can simply say: "As for me, I didn't see anything." Yes, but those who are in a position of justice must know that God has set them on high as it were in a watchtower to discover things afar off.

If the magistrates themselves put a watchman in a high tower and he excused himself, saying: "I saw nothing," will they excuse him because of that? No, for he was set there to keep watch around him; that was his duty. Even so our Lord ordains magistrates to keep a good watch. And if, despite this, they shut their eyes and pretend that they saw nothing at all, will this serve to acquit them? What kind of an excuse is that? Was there ever anything so foolish and absurd? So then let us truly remember that magistrates must keep their eyes open and be watchful in order that they may see what their duty is. And if they desire to be considered innocent, they must fulfill their duty in order that they can declare in truth: "Our eyes have not seen it, neither have our hands shed this blood."

GOD'S DEPARTURE FROM AN UNRIGHTEOUS COUNTRY

But yet, besides this, Moses shows that the city or town where a murder is committed is not wholly innocent of it, and therefore they must willingly seek pardon at God's hand. Surely this seems to be rather extreme.

"What?" it may be asked; "we have not consented to this evil, but instead we would have punished it if it had been committed in our presence. And we solemnly declare that we ourselves did not shed this blood; neither do we know the perpetrator, or we would have punished him. Shouldn't God be content with this?"

No, there is yet one more thing to be considered—namely, that the commission of such a sin defiles the whole country, and is a warning from God calling us to closely examine ourselves. It is true that He does not consider us murderers; but even so, the fact that He allowed such an offense to be committed is as though He clearly revealed to us that He has departed from us. For, when God blesses a country, He preserves it from all defilement. And the occurrence of any defilement is a sign of God's turning His back upon us as if He should say: "I will not take care of you anymore; I have let you alone and given you over."

Therefore if a nation recognizes that God has shown any signs of His displeasure to it, it truly has good reason to humble itself. And this is why He commanded the judges and governors of the city where a murder was committed to earnestly consider this, as if they should say: "Lord, have pity upon Your people Israel, and take away this shedding of innocent blood from among us, and do not allow this deed to be counted against us."

Now if it is so, and we have no remedy except to flee to God's mercy alone and to beg forgiveness not only for the sin, but also because men ought to feel that He is angry with the whole city, what is to be done when the sin is committed openly? Shouldn't men seek God all the more and make supplication to Him and flee to His mercy—at least if they were well advised? Yes, but we see what hardheartedness (or rather stupidity) is in most men nowadays—indeed, and in almost all men! For when a sin is committed, who takes notice of it? It's true that if a horribly vile wickedness is committed, men will perhaps say: "That is a wicked man." But they never consider that God warns all men individually to ask themselves: "Alas! How can it be that such a wicked crime is committed among us and all of us are defiled with it before God?"

For these crimes happen, and we never recognize that it is a sign that we have not learned or benefited from hearing God's Word. For we don't understand that He has given such examples for our instruction. But, though we might sleep, yet God does not cease to execute His office. We hear what He says when there is no justice or righteous dealing in a city: "Hear the word of the LORD, ye rulers of Sodom; give ear unto the law of our God, ye people of Gomorrah" (Is. 1:9). They are rulers of Sodom; they are thieves and murderers. He says this to judges. Not because they cut men's throats in the highway—no, but because they had not upheld the cause of the righteous and innocent (Is. 5:20, 23). Therefore He said: "the land is full of blood, and the city full of perverseness" (Eze. 9:9). The very city of Jerusalem itself, which God had chosen to be His royal palace and temple, is called a city of blood and a den of thieves. And why? Because much violence and many sins were committed there, and many poor souls were trodden under foot without relief, and justice had become open robbery.

So then, let us learn to flee to our God when any offense is committed, and let each of us say within ourselves: "Alas! Our Lord shows how angry He is with us, that such things have happened, and that such wickednesses are committed among us." Therefore let each of us beg pardon for them, and also think thus within ourselves: "Why is it that I am not like one of them? Isn't it only because of God's preservation of me?" And let us also beware for the time to come. Thus you see in effect what we must bear in mind regarding the things that are spoken here concerning murder.

THE HORROR OF SHEDDING INNOCENT BLOOD

There was also the cutting off of the heifer's head, to make men more afraid; for who cannot say that beholding such a poor beast slain in that way moves men to fear even more? And what then is to be said of a man, who is created in the image of God? We see then how our Lord meant to teach the elders and judges who were present at the sacrifice in order that they might better understand the horribleness of all murders. For if we are appalled at the slaughter of a beast, we have a much greater reason to be moved to our very bones and horrified beyond all comparison for a human creature.

Concerning the washing of their hands, this was added so that the people would understand that they were in some way defiled—or rather that they should declare that they were, both before the angels and all other creatures, that they might wash themselves from it. This act served for the time of the ceremonies of the law.

But we must understand that the giving of such a sign was not intended by our Lord to encourage His people in hypocrisy and counterfeit acting. What did Pilate gain by washing his hands? Was he absolved from the death of Jesus Christ? No. The fact that he washed his hands was a sign of his defilement. Why else would he have washed his hands except that he knew that he was guilty of the death of Jesus Christ? Therefore he thought to absolve himself by a drop of water—which was a grievous toying with God. And that is why I said that his washing stained his sin even more deeply before God and rendered him even more inexcusable.

Therefore, if the people came hypocritically to wash their hands, this would only have served to further indict them and to render themselves much guiltier. But God's desire was that the elders should use such ceremonies in order that we might better understand that we are only flesh, and that we never consider our sins as we ought to unless they are clearly pointed out to us. We never consider God's wrath until we see a very clear and evident sign of it in front of our very face. Therefore God intended to declare that when any such sin is committed, we are so defiled that there is nothing but filthiness within us. And God is so opposed to us because of it that we cannot even pray to Him without provoking Him to wrath. Mark that for one point.

STRIVING FOR CLEANNESS AND PURITY

And He also meant to show us how we ought to strive to our utmost for cleanness and purity. And this purity is not attained by corruptible water, but it must exist first in our consciences and afterwards in all our members. Therefore let us learn to see to it that our hands are not full of blood, as the prophet Isaiah calls the hands of those which did wrong to their neighbors (Is. 1:15). And let not our feet run after bloodshed, nor let our members be defiled or made instruments of unrighteousness, as Paul speaks of them (Rom. 6:13). When we in this way strive to keep ourselves undefiled toward God, then we rightly observe the washing that was required under the law, and we properly retain the truth and substance of it.

And in our day, seeing that we have baptism, the water signifies the same thing—not that it is sufficient of itself or that it has any power to wash away our sins. If it did, what would then become of the blood of our Lord Jesus Christ? It is much too great a blasphemy for a man to put his trust in a visible sign; we must raise our minds higher than that.

So also it is the same with the Lord's Supper. For, when

we come to the table of our Lord Jesus Christ, if we think we will find our soul's health in a bit of bread or in a drop of wine we are very stupid indeed, and there is neither reason nor understanding in us. But when we are further instructed, so that we understand that by eating the bread we conceive that Christ is our very sustenance; and that though we are spiritually dead in ourselves, yet we do not cease to live in Him, then the sacrament turns to our benefit. And to that use we must apply the doctrine that is set down here.

THE CRYING OUT OF INNOCENT BLOOD

And, in conclusion, let us further note that, though men who are murdered are no longer able to speak to us because they are dead, yet their blood cries out for vengeance against us. Haven't we seen what happened with the blood of Abel? He needed no attorney to plead his case, for his very blood cried out to God, as it is written (Gen. 4:10). Therefore we must understand that, even though the parties whom we have injured may forgive us, yet God will ever be a Judge against us until we have acknowledged our sins and seek to amend them. It is true that His wrath does not always appear openly against us, and that at times our wrongdoing lies concealed for a long time, so that it seems to be stark dead and quite forgotten. Yet, despite this, the remembrance of it is always fresh before God. Let us consider this, and let every one of us in true repentance rebuke himself and amend his wrongdoings, endeavoring to live quietly and without doing any harm.

And, as a greater incentive to this, let us meditate on the outcry which the Apostle mentions in his epistle to the Hebrews, saying that the blood of our Lord Jesus Christ cries much better things than did the blood of Abel (Heb. 12:24). It does not call for the vengeance of God against us if we receive Him in such a way that our sins are washed and cleansed. For this is why He shed that holy blood of His. It's true that the blood of our Lord Jesus Christ will cry out for vengeance against all unbelievers and wicked men and against all who have scorned the teaching of the Gospel and have trodden it underfoot and have made a mockery of it, and all profane folks, for all these will be guilty of the innocent blood of our Lord Jesus Christ.

But when we receive His blood by faith and know that it will serve us as a propitiation to make us righteous and innocent before God, let us rest assured that this same blood has its cry. And indeed we see how the Gospel sounds and rings in our ears in order that we might know the power of the blood of our Lord Jesus Christ. For it is no dead thing, but it is always fresh, as the Apostle speaks of it in another place (Heb. 10:10). Yes, and it is so fresh that it eternally possesses His living power to reconcile us to God. Therefore let us properly consider this inestimable blessing, and receive the peace of the Gospel by which God declares to us that He accepts the blood of His Son for our cleansing, that we may appear before His majesty with full hope.

Now let us cast ourselves down in the presence of our good God with acknowledgement of our faults, praying Him to make us perceive them more and more. Yes, and let us confess not only the sins that we ourselves are aware of and perceive, and of which we ought to be ashamed before men; but also our sins of ignorance and our secret sins of which we are now guilty. And, because we know how many vices and infirmities there are within us, let us mourn them before God, and let this ever make us walk more and more in true repentance.

And in the meanwhile let us not continue willfully in sin, but let us take courage to turn to Him. And let us not seek a bullock or a brute beast to answer for us nowadays, as though its blood could serve us for a sacrifice, but let us flee to our Lord Jesus Christ, seeing that He has offered up the only and the everlasting sacrifice in His death and passion once for all, to set us free from all our debts, and that He calls us daily to Himself by His Gospel. Let us seek no other means to serve God, but proceed in all purity under His hand and guidance. And may it please Him to grant this grace not only to us, but also to all people and nations of the earth.

Letters of Comfort to the Persecuted Church

by Pierre Viret
translated by R. A. Sheats

Softcover, 114 pages
ISBN: 978-1-938822-50-6

From the depths of a pastor's heart come letters of hearty biblical comfort for persecuted believers. Written to men and women facing imprisonment, banishment, suffering, and death, these letters capture the heart of the Gospel and offer consolation and sincere comfort for those suffering for the sake of Christ.

Written by Pierre Viret (1511-1571), a Swiss Reformer and close friend of John Calvin, these letters overflow with a pastoral concern for the souls as well as the physical needs of his readers. Republished several times throughout the Reformation era, Viret's letters appear now for the first time in the English language, and the comfort they offer to an afflicted church is as pertinent today as it was the day he wrote them.

PIERRE VIRET:
The Angel of the Reformation

by R. A. Sheats

Hardcover, 323 pages
ISBN: 978-098437817

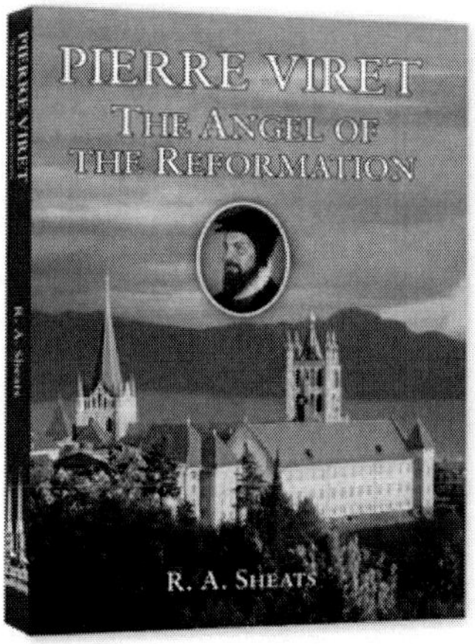

For the first time in five hundred years, a full biography of Pierre Viret is now available to the English-speaking world. Packed with fascinating details and bristling with original documents and letters of the Reformers, the history of this forgotten giant of the Reformation is recounted in an interesting and enthralling way. Known by his contemporaries as *the Angel of the Reformation*, Viret was truly a radiant light amongst the men of his generation, a light which has finally been uncovered in this our day. May the unveiling of this precious life inspire and equip a new generation of Reformers as they seek to extend God's glory to every area of human existence!

"R. A. has written a superb biography on our Swiss Reformer that is both warmhearted and scholarly. We anticipate a soon translation into French."

- **Daniel Bovet**, President of *l'Association Pierre Viret*, Switzerland

Made in United States
North Haven, CT
04 November 2026

21772484R00067